PRAISE FOR JOSH FECHTER
& HIS WORKS

"Do what Josh Fechter tells you to...I stumbled on The Copwriting Bible last weekend thought I'd try it. My last two posts on Linkedin—having done nothing more than copy-and-pasting, editing them a bit to make them my own and throwing them out there—had more than 137,000 views in 2 days. Use this book."
— AARON ORENDORFF, EDITOR-IN-CHIEF AT SHOPIFY PLUS, FOUNDER OF INCONICONTENT

"Bottom line, [Josh Fechter] creates tremendous value for people, they see a clear benefit to associating with him."
— DENNIS YU, CTO OF BLITZMETRICS

"Knowing cool growth hacks doesn't make you a great marketer. Josh also practices what he preaches, both for his own brand and for various clients."
— JULIUS BARON, FOUNDER OF JUMPKIT

THE
COPYWRITING
BIBLE

100 + VIRAL OUTLINES
TO BUILD YOUR BRAND

THE
COPY
WRITING
BIBLE

JOSH FECHTER

PEACH ELEPHANT PRESS

This book is designed to provide information that the author believes to be accurate on the subject matter it covers, and is written from the author's personal experience. In the text that follows, many people's and company's names and identifying characteristics have been changed, so that any resemblance to actual persons, living or dead, events, companies or locales is entirely coincidental.

Any references to resources and materials produced by other entities are purely the author's own interpretation. The author does not imply an endorsement from any of the sources cited within this book.

ISBN 978-0-9951103-8-0 (HARDCOVER)

First Printing, 2018
Peach Elephant Press

CONTENTS

INTRODUCTION

After I released the first copywriting outline, I watched sixty copycat posts go viral. This is when I knew releasing a hundred more would break the pendulum, the balance of what was.

Would it change the way society fundamentally looked at writing?

Would it change the way people interact online forever?

All it takes is several.

Several people to nail down this style. If I inspire only three writers to pursue this craft every day, the reach of the book will affect millions, if not, billions. It had to happen. Waiting became no longer an option.

I didn't understand the impact a book like this could have until my roommate at the time, Jacobie Jane, laughed about it. She recognized that the book had nothing to do with my writing. It had everything to do with breaking the norms.

She said, "Women have been writing poetry like this forever. It's only because you made it popular for men, do people care. And most importantly, you're using it to sell." She was right.

I was among the first young men to make it culturally acceptable for other men to write vulnerable content. Content about failure, rejection, and hardship. This content isn't new. Young men had written this way before, but few to the extent I had. Close to a thousand pieces over the span of several years.

Then I realized it wasn't just men - it was women. Women founders scared to share their voice in a male-dominated entrepreneurial culture. Because even though women had written this way before, it never made itself a forefront in their entrepreneurial careers.

As a result of my writing, something remarkable happened.

I created a movement.

A community.

A force to be reckoned with.

In a short time, my writing took me from a little-known entrepreneur to the big stage. Over 2017, I was one of the most-viewed writers on LinkedIn. I received Top Quora Writer of 2017 & 2018 awards. I reached over 200 million people with content and created a strong community of 19,000+ marketers and founders. Then I used this audience to scale my company from 0 to 26 employees in 8 months on track for several million dollars in revenue the first year.

The audience helped us recruit most of our initial employees and customers. It pushed a little-known company, **BAMF** Media, into the limelight forced to fit into its brand as Reuters, Forbes, Entrepreneur, Mashable, Inc., and BuzzFeed covered our work. It meant my co-founder, Houston Golden, and I would need to brace ourselves for growth, stay nimble, and test fast. That's exactly what we did, and it paid off big.

My co-founder and I were nominated by Forbes as "12 Innovative Founders to Watch." I was given opportunities to speak at Growth

Marketing Conference, Traction Conference, Startup Grind Global, and **SXSW**. And have such an incredible journey, it'd provide me the opportunity to write several books about my learning experiences: **THE BAMF BIBLE**, LinkedIn Influencer, and Content Machine.

Here's what people don't see: The origin didn't begin with the result of money and a following in mind. I'd written more vulnerable content soon after graduating college. My parents had gone through a divorce, my family relationships were broken, and I was off trying to become a successful entrepreneur, but failing at every turn. Eight failed startups.

I had nothing, but pain.

I needed a way to release it.

To tell someone.

As my release, I wrote statuses on Facebook, Quora, and LinkedIn. Statuses with stories detailing my pain. This pain turned into an understanding, a common bond with an audience, and a rightful passage of trust because I had nothing to hide about my journey.

The twist: After years of writing this type of content, I can write almost about anything and make it interesting. This gives me the ability to write about my company without the audience ever feeling like they're getting sold to. Today, it's the most powerful skill in online marketing, building a brand, and becoming a company that's not a product or service, but a movement.

It's on LinkedIn:

It's on Facebook:

It's on Quora:

Many of these stories are re-posted across multiple platforms with zero alteration.

Because the platform doesn't change the impact of the stories. Only the writing does. I've reused the same story countless times to reach millions and millions of more people.

In business verticals where companies have historically relied on paid advertising, there's a movement happening. It's content marketing through storytelling. Not in the way you're used to it with blog articles detailing case studies. Instead, these are deep, vulnerable stories about who we are.

Through these stories and outlines, you'll see just how anyone can push through the noise of online marketing to stand out. Best yet, how you can do it too. Not all of these stories are mine, but I have inspired almost all of them.

The structure of the outlines included in this book are mobile optimized. It's not required to *pop*.

As the same writing works in several-line spurts:

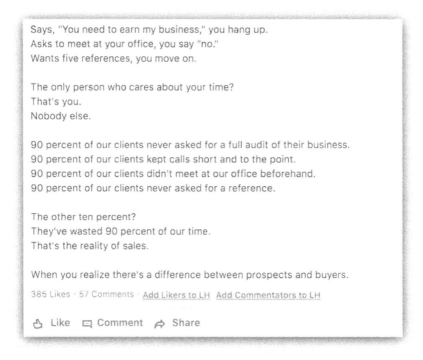

And in chunks:

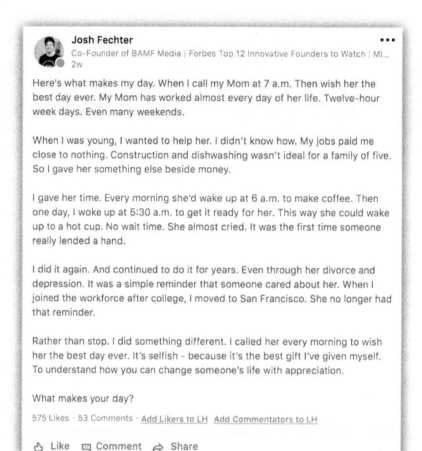

Josh Fechter
Co-Founder of BAMF Media | Forbes Top 12 Innovative Founders to Watch | Mi...
2w

Here's what makes my day. When I call my Mom at 7 a.m. Then wish her the best day ever. My Mom has worked almost every day of her life. Twelve-hour week days. Even many weekends.

When I was young, I wanted to help her. I didn't know how. My jobs paid me close to nothing. Construction and dishwashing wasn't ideal for a family of five. So I gave her something else beside money.

I gave her time. Every morning she'd wake up at 6 a.m. to make coffee. Then one day, I woke up at 5:30 a.m. to get it ready for her. This way she could wake up to a hot cup. No wait time. She almost cried. It was the first time someone really lended a hand.

I did it again. And continued to do it for years. Even through her divorce and depression. It was a simple reminder that someone cared about her. When I joined the workforce after college, I moved to San Francisco. She no longer had that reminder.

Rather than stop. I did something different. I called her every morning to wish her the best day ever. It's selfish - because it's the best gift I've given myself. To understand how you can change someone's life with appreciation.

What makes your day?

575 Likes · 53 Comments · Add Likers to LH   Add Commentators to LH

👍 Like   💬 Comment   ➦ Share

The most important part about all these pieces?

It's the tangibility. You can feel the emotion of the story.

In these hundred outlines, you'll realize just how you can transfer that emotion to the reader. All while genuinely telling the story of your company in almost every piece. If you're ready to understand storytelling copy, then let's break the internet.

100+ VIRAL OUTLINES TO BUILD YOUR BRAND

HOW TO USE THESE OUTLINES

The first part of each template will contain a social media status I have written. The next few pages after that will have a set of rules to follow for your own posts, a reminder of my example, and a space for you to brainstorm ideas for what you might write about.

You can either:

1. Jot down some ideas, a few words, and flesh them out later on your computer.
2. Write a full sentence or two that you think will work there for your own post.

Enjoy the process, and I hope this workbook helps you plan out many viral posts.

MAJOR CHANGE
TO PURSUE YOUR DREAM

I left to a new city.

I took a fifty percent pay cut.

I needed a way to dive deep into the tech world to find my kin.

When I made it to San Francisco, I felt like I had taken my first big step in accomplishing my dream of building a high-caliber team.

A year and a half later, I found my co-founder, Houston Golden.

Not in San Francisco, but in Los Angeles.

He's the smartest growth guy I know having experience of managing up to twenty clients at once in viral marketing to ridiculous amounts of ad spend.

I interviewed hundreds of marketers and founders to find him.

It takes patience.

And when you find your teammate, it's important you sacrifice to make them a part of your team. For me, I moved to Los Angeles a week later.

A month later, we've officially moved into our new office in Santa Monica.

Start with a major change:

I left to a new city.

Dig into the pain:

I took a fifty percent pay cut.

Because I needed a way to make the right relationships:

I needed a way to dive deep into the tech world to find my kin.

When it happened, I could tell I had finally jumped into my mission:

When I made it to San Francisco, I felt like I had taken my first big step in accomplishing my dream of building a high-caliber team.

— It took a lot of time before I found my next step: —

A year and a half later, I found my co-founder, Houston Golden.

— And it wasn't where I expected it: —

Not in San Francisco, but in Los Angeles.

— It made sense because of these tangible benefits: —

He's the smartest growth guy I know having experience of managing up to twenty clients at once in viral marketing to ridiculous amounts of ad spend.

— It took this tangible hard work to find this step: —

I interviewed hundreds of marketers and founders to find him.

— Here's my learning: —

It takes patience.

When you find that step, then do whatever you can to take it. For me, this meant taking X life change:

And when you find your teammate, it's important you sacrifice to make them a part of your team. For me, I moved to Los Angeles a week later.

I made it happen fast - and now here I am:

A month later, we've officially moved into our new office in Santa Monica.

CRITICISMS IN THE FACE OF FEAR

"Your company name is childish."

"I can't take you seriously with that LinkedIn profile photo."

"The phrase 'growth hacker' is for people who don't understand marketing."

I get these comments every day.

I love them.

They add fuel to my fire.

It's easy to feel bullied once you start posting lots of content on LinkedIn.

People attack you in the comments left and right without offering solutions.

I'm not perfect.

I'm an early-stage founder.

I'm discovering new weaknesses every day.

I'm using this platform to be entirely transparent about my business, so I can get constructive feedback and make genuine connections.

This means sharing failures and successes.

So, when you decide to bash me because of a failure, realize I'm not an expert at hiring or simply being human. I'm trying.

And for the millions who take a step forward every day in the face criticism, I respect you.

Highlight several tangible criticisms you receive to make yourself vulnerable:

"Your company name is childish."
"I can't take you seriously with that LinkedIn profile photo."
"The phrase 'growth hacker' is for people who don't understand marketing."

This happens often:

I get these comments every day.

I keep a positive response:

I love them.

I turn this negative into a positive outcome:

They add fuel to my fire.

It's easy to feel down on yourself when you choose to stand out:

It's easy to feel bullied once you start posting lots of content on LinkedIn.

Haters will come after you in waves:

People attack you in the comments left and right without offering solutions.

I make mistakes:

I'm not perfect.

I know this is why:

I'm an early-stage founder.

I'm finding more problems every day:

I'm discovering new weaknesses every day.

That's why I'm open about them in front of you guys all the time - just like now:

I'm using this platform to be entirely transparent about my business, so I can get constructive feedback and make genuine connections.

It means I have to take the extra step of being vulnerable in this way:

This means sharing failures and successes.

If you decide to come after me because of a weakness, then realize I'm still learning:

So, when you decide to bash me because of a failure, realize I'm not an expert at hiring or simply being human.
I'm trying.

Not only me, but many others face the same obstacles. I look at them in a positive way:

And for the millions who take a step forward every day in the face criticism, I respect you.

WHY I'VE ONLY CHOSEN THIS ROUTE

I've only worked for startups.

However, I've had moments where I was sitting at a laptop and applied to hundreds of big brand companies.

I've never made the jump, but I know why I sent out my resume.

I felt tired.

Tired of seeing a low bank account balance.

Tired of coming to work where everyone is on edge.

Tired of working months on a project with a high probability of failure.

Tired of not seeing my girlfriend for weeks at a time because I'm working too much.

It takes a toll.

It can feel like you're suffocating.

You gasp for air, but there's nothing there.

You look at people who work for corporate companies. You see their pictures on Facebook of them going on vacation, hanging out at the beach with their girlfriend, and attending conferences.

Not you.

You're in your empty office on a Saturday night working until 3 a.m.

You feel very alone, but you tell yourself it's worth it.

I can be a part of something great.

I can say, "I was there from the beginning. I helped build it."

You continue working because you believe in creating a great legacy.

You believe passion and perseverance will conquer all obstacles.

You believe in yourself.

I've only done X:

I've only worked for startups.

It doesn't mean I haven't thought about the opposite:

However, I've had moments where I was sitting at a laptop and applied to hundreds of big brand companies.

It never happened, but I still dipped my toes in:

I've never made the jump, but I know why I sent out my resume.

I did it because of the pain:

I felt tired.

Four tangible examples:

Tired of seeing a low bank account balance.
Tired of coming to work where everyone is on edge.
Tired of working months on a project with a high probability of failure.
Tired of not seeing my girlfriend for weeks at a time because I'm working too much.

It's not easy:

It takes a toll.

── It feels like this imaginary tangible example: ──

It can feel like you're suffocating.

── Dig into the pain: ──

You gasp for air, but there's nothing there.

── You don't experience all the fun other people get to have: ──

You look at people who work for corporate companies. You see their pictures on Facebook of them going on vacation, hanging out at the beach with their girlfriend, and attending conferences.

── You're left out in the dust: ──

Not you.

You're doing the exact opposite — something miserable:

You're in your empty office on a Saturday night working until 3 a.m.

It's hard, but you have hope:

You feel very alone, but you tell yourself it's worth it.

Because of the legacy:

I can be a part of something great.

And for this specific moment:

I can say, "I was there from the beginning. I helped build it."

You keep pushing forward because of these three beliefs:

You continue working because you believe in creating a great legacy.
You believe passion and perseverance will conquer all obstacles.
You believe in yourself.

SCARED TO TAKE ACTION BECAUSE OF MY TITLE

As an employee, I didn't post a lot on LinkedIn. I was scared.

"What if I lose my job over a statement management takes the wrong way?"

When I became a founder, I broke free of my chains and began posting more.

Something remarkable happened: I received hundreds of opportunities.

I realized founders should encourage their employees to post more—to share their experiences.

Why?

Their company would generate more leads.

Their company would stand out amongst their competition.

Their company would develop more trust through a transparent culture.

The most untapped potential of a company lies within the voice of their employees, especially on LinkedIn.

Give them reign to what they've always deserved: Their opinion.

I didn't do this one common practice because of my title:

As an employee, I didn't post a lot on LinkedIn.
I was scared.

Self-conscious thought

"What if I lose my job over a statement management takes the wrong way?"

A big life change happened, I no longer had fear. I could take action:

When I became a founder, I broke free of my chains and began posting more.

This action led to great results:

Something remarkable happened: I received hundreds of opportunities.

We need to combat the self-conscious thoughts from
branding titles:

I realized founders should encourage their employees to post more—to share
their experiences.
Why?

You'd get these tangible benefits:

Their company would generate more leads.
Their company would stand out amongst their competition.
Their company would develop more trust through a transparent culture.

Say a statement everyone can agree with, then tie it
into the overall picture and make it relevant to the
common action setting:

The most untapped potential of a company lies within the voice of their
employees, especially on LinkedIn.

Dig deeper into this confirmation bias statement:

Give them reign to what they've always deserved:
Their opinion.

WHEN I WAS X
I KNEW TWO THINGS

When I was twenty-two years old, I knew two things:
1. I wasn't happy with my career.
2. I would do anything and everything to find happiness.

In the span of five years, I went through ten startups and moved eight times.

Each startup and place I lived were better than the last.

I could've settled, but I demanded more from life. I followed my gut and took calculated risks. I never waited.

I canceled out all of these negative thoughts:

"What if my co-workers get upset because I leave?"

"How will this company survive without me?"

"Will my friends hate me if I no longer talk to them as much?"

Stop it.

I've seen friends stay at their miserable job for five years because they're scared the company will fail without them. That's insane.

As a twenty-two year old, the chances are you don't have a lot of responsibility. It's the perfect time to take risks.

It's so much harder once you have a significant other and kids, and have to take care of your parents because they've grown old.

You have a choice to do anything in life right now. There are over seven billion people to connect with, and close to two hundred countries filled with opportunity.

Don't waste a second doing something you don't enjoy.

Nothing is obligatory.

You must move fast to find what you love.

Lead into a realization:

When I was twenty-two years old, I knew two things:

A painful one:

1. I wasn't happy with my career.

With some hope:

2. I would do anything and everything to find happiness.

This hope led me to have a wild life:

In the span of five years, I went through ten startups and moved eight times.

I discovered progress:

Each startup and place I lived were better than the last.

Sure, I could've been like everyone else, but I wanted more so I took risks by doing X & Y:

I could've settled, but I demanded more from life. I followed my gut and took calculated risks. I never waited.

To make it happen, I had to not do X:

I canceled out all of these negative thoughts:

That included these tangible thoughts:

"What if my co-workers get upset because I leave?"
"How will this company survive without me?"
"Will my friends hate me if I no longer talk to them as much?"

You can't do this:

Stop it.

Otherwise this will happen to you down the road:

*I've seen friends stay at their miserable job for five years because they're scared the company will fail without them. **That's insane**.*

When you have this advantage, it's the best time to chase your dreams:

As a twenty-two year old, the chances are you don't have a lot of responsibility. It's the perfect time to take risks.

Don't wait until this tangible example happens, then it's too late:

It's so much harder once you have a significant other and kids, and have to take care of your parents because they've grown old.

The time is now. Here's a tangible example to help you see the bigger picture:

You have a choice to do anything in life right now. There are over seven billion people to connect with, and close to two hundred countries filled with opportunity.

Move forward:

Don't waste a second doing something you don't enjoy. Nothing is obligatory.

To discover what you need:

You must move fast to find what you love.

KEEPING YOUR PROMISES

We had a handshake deal on a non-compete agreement for a client.

Several days later, a competitor stepped on our toes with 10X more revenue wanting to work with us.

"Houston, I know we said we wouldn't work with anyone else."

"Josh, that's true. I wasn't expecting this."

As a startup with revenue that could always be higher, it's hard to turn down opportunities.

I would be lying if I said I didn't think about taking the deal.

After all, we didn't sign anything.

Then I remembered what my Dad says,

"In business, nothing hurts you more than lying."

I made the executive decision to keep our handshake deal because I know trust is earned.

Could we have grown our team by taking the bigger deal?

Sure. And a bigger office wouldn't hurt.

As the co-founder of **BAMF** Media, I know we're in the game for the long run.

When we commit to something—even if it's a handshake—we honor it.

Running a successful business is not about the amount of revenue you close.

It's about the culture you inspire.

And moments like this one define it.

I made a business promise:

We had a handshake deal on a non-compete agreement for a client.

I got offered a better opportunity soon after that'd break my promise:

Several days later, a competitor stepped on our toes with 10X more revenue wanting to work with us.

Tangible conversation moment:

"Houston, I know we said we wouldn't work with anyone else."
"Josh, that's true. I wasn't expecting this."

From a vanity perspective, it made sense for us to chase it:

As a startup with revenue that could always be higher, it's hard to turn down opportunities.

We thought about it:

I would be lying if I said I didn't think about taking the deal. After all, we didn't sign anything.

Then I remembered my principles:

Then I remembered what my Dad says, "In business, nothing hurts you more than lying."

I kept my business promise:

I made the executive decision to keep our handshake deal because I know trust is earned.

We might've missed out on all these tangible benefits:

Could we have grown our team by taking the bigger deal?
Sure.
And a bigger office wouldn't hurt.

But culture and principles are more important, especially with my position:

As the co-founder of BAMF Media, I know we're in the game for the long run.
When we commit to something—even if it's a handshake—we
honor it.

It's about the bigger picture:

Running a successful business is not about the amount of revenue
you close.
It's about the culture you inspire.

Tie the story back:

And moments like this one define it.

HUGE LIFE CHANGE ON A GUT FEELING

My co-founder convinced me to move to Los Angeles to start a media agency.

It took him three hours and a couple of beers to win me over.

And I had never met him in person before that night.

There are a few moments in life where you meet people who inspire you to work next to them.

The problem: These moments are disguised with pain.

I'd leave one of the best jobs in tech.

I'd move to a new city with no network.

I'd have to solidify our service offerings to attract clients.

All for what?

To work with someone I had a beer with for several hours?

What I've learned: Obstacles will always be there.

The right people won't.

When you find them — hang on.

It's never the money that makes opportunities worth chasing.

It's the people.

Thanks Houston for inspiring greatness into everyone around you.

If you hadn't, **BAMF** Media would never exist.

— Big life change because of an individual: ——

My co-founder convinced me to move to Los Angeles to start a media agency.

— Decided in a short period: ——

It took him three hours and a couple of beers to win me over.

— With almost zero evidence: ——

And I had never met him in person before that night.

— Sometimes you need to dare greatly: ——

There are a few moments in life where you meet people who inspire you to work next to them.

It's hard to see the opportunity because of everything you'll leave behind:

The problem: These moments are disguised with pain.
I'd leave one of the best jobs in tech.
I'd move to a new city with no network.
I'd have to solidify our service offerings to attract clients.

It never makes sense to jump:

All for what?
To work with someone I had a beer with for several hours?

Here's why you do it:

What I've learned: Obstacles will always be there.
The right people won't.
When you find them - hang on.

Don't focus on vanity. Focus on what matters:

It's never the money that makes opportunities worth chasing.
It's the people.

Thank the individual mentioned in #1:

Thanks Houston for inspiring greatness into everyone around you. If you hadn't, BAMF Media would never exist.

SURVIVED A HARD TIME
BECAUSE OF THIS HABIT

I survived hell week.

Entirely drained, I took a nap on the floor of my office (we don't have couches yet) and woke up a minute ago to write this.

This week, we announced the launch of our agency, moved into our new office, and co-hosted our first LA BAMF event.

We booked many sales calls from referrals, conducted a few webinars, and built out a large part of our website.

Many people ask me how I have time for life balance.

It's simple — I avoid pointless sales conversations.

The first question I ask every person who wants to work with our agency:

"What's your marketing budget?"

For advising and consulting, I state my price in the first reply.

I rather not talk to someone for an hour to realize they can't afford our services. It's a waste of our time.

Most people don't do this because they're afraid to scare people off with their pricing.

The truth is you should want to scare people off with your pricing.

Because the right people will stay.

On the other side, this is one of the fastest ways to understand whether someone knows their shit.

If they don't state their price immediately, then they don't value their time.

I often find myself the only person in a room who's willing to admit how much money they've lost and are making.

This is why people trust me.

I overcame an obstacle:

I survived hell week.

The problem and time relevance:

Entirely drained, I took a nap on the floor of my office (we don't have couches yet) and woke up a minute ago to write this.

This problem exists because we're doing well with these tangible examples:

This week, we announced the launch of our agency, moved into our new office, and co-hosted our first LA BAMF event.

Even more tangible examples:

We booked many sales calls from referrals, conducted a few webinars, and built out a large part of our website.

Many people wonder how this can happen:

Many people ask me how I have time for life balance.

I hold this one tangible principle true:

It's simple — I avoid pointless sales conversations.
The first question I ask every person who wants to work with our agency: "What's your marketing budget?"
For advising and consulting, I state my price in the first reply.

I do this to avoid these negative outcomes:

I rather not talk to someone for an hour to realize they can't afford our services. It's a waste of our time.

Most people don't because of this reason:

Most people don't do this because they're afraid to scare people off with their pricing.

Here's the truth of why that's wrong - with a benefit:

The truth is you should want to scare people off with your pricing. Because the right people will stay.

Here's another unseen benefit:

On the other side, this is one of the fastest ways to understand whether someone knows their shit.

This is why:

If they don't state their price immediately, then they don't value their time.

Sometimes I'm among the few:

I often find myself the only person in a room who's willing to admit how much money they've lost and are making.

As a result, this positive benefit happens:

This is why people trust me.

I PAID MY DUES TO GET HERE

I get it.

I'm a young founder.

I'm always willing to listen, but if you say I still need to "earn" my success, then you're wrong.

I can't count the number of times people have said this.

I went through eight failed startups as an intern, founder, and head of growth.

I've lost tens of thousands of dollars in bad social media and stock investments.

I've learned from my mistakes.

After my early failures, I've led growth at several successful companies

And I used my community to help grow over one thousand companies this year alone. I get thank-you messages every day.

And still, "well-respected" people in the industry tell me I haven't "earned" it.

As a twenty-six-year-old founder, I've learned the only respect I need to earn is my own.

People will always find a reason to knock you, especially if they're jealous.

Let them focus on you.

Then ignore them to focus on the people you're helping.

Lead them into a vulnerable part of who you are:

I get it.

The vulnerability:

I'm a young founder.

I stay humble, but don't tell me I still need to overcome certain obstacles:

I'm always willing to listen, but if you say I still need to "earn" my success, then you're wrong.

Many people do this:

I can't count the number of times people have said this.

I had my learning experiences through these tangible failures:

I went through eight failed startups as an intern, founder, and head of growth. I've lost tens of thousands of dollars in bad social media and stock investments.

— I've earned it: ————————————————————————

I've learned from my mistakes.

— Because I grew as a person. This is shown with these —
  tangible results:

After my early failures, I've led growth at several successful companies
And I used my community to help grow over one thousand companies this year
alone. I get thank-you messages every day.

— Doesn't matter how many people you help. There will —
  always be influencers who doubt you:

And still, "well-respected" people in the industry tell me I haven't "earned" it.

— The truth is the only opinion that matters is my own: —

As a twenty-six-year-old founder, I've learned the only respect I need to earn is
my own.

— There will always be haters: ————————————————

People will always find a reason to knock you, especially if they're jealous.

They'll stay distracted while you'll keep winning:

Let them focus on you.
Then ignore them to focus on the people you're helping.

I TOOK A DUMB OPPORTUNITY THEN CAME UP

I had the opportunity to work with people from Google, McKinsey, and Amazon.

We had a startup: "Tinder for Jobs"

I came from a state school and recently left my failed startup, so I felt blessed for the opportunity.

During this time, I had a mentor, Scott Case, co-founder of Priceline.

I sent him a cold email after I saw him speaking at a conference. I told him I'd try to offer him value even as a recent college graduate.

The ask? Grab a quick coffee.

When I met him for coffee, I showed him the company's mobile app.

"It's going to fail."

Harsh.

Then, it got worse.

"Josh, I want you to know something. When it comes to startups, no one has any idea about what he or she is doing. It doesn't matter what company or college they came from." It's true.

None of us knew how to find product/market fit or get traction.

We felt stuck.

Losing more users every day.

Seeing our runway decrease every day.

It turns out, we didn't understand "growth," the systematic approach to solving problems to help a startup get traction.

For the next several years, I devoted my life to figure it out. It's no coincidence that today, I work with thousands of startups to help them grow.

As long as we decide to rise from the ashes, we can lend a hand to help others do so as well.

Start with an incredible opportunity with credible names:

I had the opportunity to work with people from Google, McKinsey, and Amazon.

Make the work funny and/or ironic:

We had a startup: "Tinder for Jobs"

It doesn't matter because the opportunity was given to you after a failure:

I came from a state school and recently left my failed startup, so I felt blessed for the opportunity.

At this time, you had help from a credible source:

During this time, I had a mentor, Scott Case, co-founder of Priceline.

I got this credible source to help me through hustle:

I sent him a cold email after I saw him speaking at a conference. I told him I'd try to offer him value even as a recent college graduate.

Here's how I got this source:

The ask? Grab a quick coffee.

I showed them my work:

When I met him for coffee, I showed him the company's mobile app.

The harsh feedback on our work with a tangible example:

"It's going to fail."
Harsh.

Dig the knife in with a tangible example of further feedback:

Then, it got worse.
"Josh, I want you to know something. When it comes to startups, no one has any idea about what he or she is doing. It doesn't matter what company or college they came from."

They were right:

It's true.
None of us knew how to find product/market fit or get traction.

As a result, we came across these problems at our work:

We felt stuck. Losing more users every day. Seeing our runway decrease every day.

We realized we were missing a fundamental principle:

It turns out, we didn't understand "growth," the systematic approach to solving problems to help a startup get traction.

So, I decided to spend an extended period figuring it out. As a result, this positive outcome happened:

For the next several years, I devoted my life to figure it out. It's no coincidence that today, I work with thousands of startups to help them grow.

Bad things happen—it's up to us to overcome them to help others:

As long as we decide to rise from the ashes, we can lend a hand to help others do so as well.

I SET THE TONE FOR
MY COMPANY CULTURE

It's hard.

Waking up at 4:30 a.m.

Going to sleep before 9 p.m.

I set the tone with my routine.

As a young company, there's one variable that matters more than every other one: culture.

The right culture can keep employees healthy; discover product/market fit; and move mountains of problems when all seems lost.

My co-founder reminded me last night, "It starts now."

"If we want a culture where people enjoy working here, we need to go home earlier and focus on our health.

They model their lives after us.

Let's make sure we're happy, so they're happy."

We can get caught up in building a business by working long hours, then burn out.

Or, we can caught up in building a legacy.

That requires longevity. And that requires happiness.

Hit them with a vague pain statement:

It's hard.

Here's what's painful:

Waking up at 4:30 a.m.
Going to sleep before 9 p.m.

I do it because it makes me a leader:

I set the tone with my routine.

Here's why:

As a young company, there's one variable that matters more than every other one: culture.
The right culture can keep employees healthy; discover product/market fit; and move mountains of problems when all seems lost.

I had a tangible reminder recently:

My co-founder reminded me last night, "It starts now."
"If we want a culture where people enjoy working here, we need to go home earlier and focus on our health.

People follow what we do:

They model their lives after us.

So let's be at our best:

Let's make sure we're happy, so they're happy."

We have these two tangible options:

We can get caught up in building a business by working long hours, then burn out. Or, we can caught up in building a legacy.

The positive ones require these attributes:

That requires longevity. And that requires happiness.

TAKE ACTION NOW

I fired myself from ten different jobs.

I never waited until my hiring manager did it for me.

And I never lined up another job.

As soon as it *clicked* that I wasn't learning, I didn't spend another day chasing a dead end.

When I didn't get feedback from executives, I fired myself.

When I realized our startup didn't have product/market fit, I fired myself.

When management wouldn't give me permission to pursue new marketing channels, I left to found **BAMF** Media.

Life is too short.

That job you want to line up before you jump ship?

That may take another three months of you listening to executives who ignore every one of your opinions.

Stop it.

If you wait to get fired, you're reacting to life.

If you fire yourself, then you're acting on life.

The right time to be happy and grow as an individual is never yesterday.

It's always now.

─── I grabbed the wheel on my future: ───────

I fired myself from ten different jobs.

─── Before they did it for me: ───────

I never waited until my hiring manager did it for me.

─── I didn't wait for a plan B: ───────

And I never lined up another job.

─── As soon as it hit me, I was gone: ───────

As soon as it *clicked* that I wasn't learning, I didn't spend another day chasing a dead end.

─── Here are the tangible moments: ───────

When I didn't get feedback from executives, I fired myself.
When I realized our startup didn't have product/market fit, I fired myself.
When management wouldn't give me permission to pursue new marketing channels, I left to found BAMF Media.

Primary reason:

Life is too short.

That other option?

That job you want to line up before you jump ship?

You don't deserve the pain of waiting:

That may take another three months of you listening to executives who ignore every one of your opinions.
Stop it.

Take control of your life:

If you wait to get fired, you're reacting to life.
If you fire yourself, then you're acting on life.

The right moment is always now:

The right time to be happy and grow as an individual is never yesterday.
It's always now.

THE BEST THANK YOU
IS DOING THE SAME FOR OTHERS

"What's your business model?"

"How will you hire new employees?"

I had no idea what I was doing when I founded my agency from an operations standpoint.

But I knew three things:
1. I can get clients excellent results.
2. I can generate hundreds of inbound leads.
3. I can find the right mentors to help me skip over early mistakes.

By chance, one of the people I met who saved me years of struggle was Aaron Agius, the founder of one of the most well-renowned content marketing agencies.

He works with the largest brands, including Coca-Cola.

I looked at him as a hero.

And he looked at me as a young, inspired entrepreneur who needed a hand.

Over the next several weeks of scaling my agency, he took his time to walk me past many problems that would have dug our agency into a ditch.

I offered him equity, time, and anything else he wanted in appreciation for his effort.

He replied, "This is what I do. I like your team. I'm here to build the right relationships. I don't need a thank you."

People like Aaron Agius are why successful entrepreneurs exist.

They're willing to help because relationships underlie everything we have.

They're in the industry for the right reasons.

The best thank-you I can give is doing the same for others.

Start the piece with the problem in a conversational tone:

"What's your business model?"
"How will you hire new employees?"

Tie it into your story and problem:

I had no idea what I was doing when I founded my agency from an operations standpoint.

I had a bit of hope with these tangible examples:

But I knew three things:
1. I can get clients excellent results.
2. I can generate hundreds of inbound leads.
3. I can find the right mentors to help me skip over early mistakes.

— Tie the last bit of hope into who you're appreciating — and drop some credibility about them:

By chance, one of the people I met who saved me years of struggle was Aaron Agius, the founder of one of the most well-renowned content marketing agencies.

— Insert tangible credibility: —————————

He works with the largest brands, including Coca-Cola.

— Why they're important to you: —————————

I looked at him as a hero.

— They decided to help someone who needed it: —————

And he looked at me as a young, inspired entrepreneur who needed a hand.

— How did they help you in a positive way (scaling — agency) and avoid negative pitfalls (dug our agency into a ditch):

Over the next several weeks of scaling my agency, he took his time to walk me past many problems that would have dug our agency into a ditch.

— I tried to repay them, but all they wanted was to help: —

I offered him equity, time, and anything else he wanted in appreciation for his effort.

— Tangible conversational response: —

He replied, "This is what I do. I like your team. I'm here to build the right relationships. I don't need a thank you."

— People like this are why we have hope for [X]: —

People like Aaron Agius are why successful entrepreneurs exist.

— Reiterate the why: —

They're willing to help because relationships underlie everything we have. They're in the industry for the right reasons.

— The result is I can do this for others: —

The best thank-you I can give is doing the same for others.

I HAD AN ACCOMPLISHMENT
BUT REALIZED THIS WAS A FASTER WAY

I read one-hundred-and-twenty-books in a year.

I documented the entire process online.

And I learned something valuable: Execution matters more.

I began to read non-stop when two of my startups failed.

I lost all my money.

I wanted to know why this happened to me.

Because my resume looked like chopped liver, I took a job as a low-paid copywriter.

Eight months later, I looked up from the pages and realized: I'm still fucken broke.

I stopped reading and took another risk. I took a pay cut from my already low-paid copywriter job to work at a Facebook software startup on contract.

The co-founders took their time to mentor me. Eventually, I worked my way up and became their head of growth.

We became the first company to live stream on Facebook.

With a month and a half of mentorship, I learned more than I did from reading the one-hundred-and-twenty books.

Why? I jumped into the unknown.

You won't find the answers to life in a book.

You'll find them living outside your comfort zone.

— I had this huge accomplishment according to most — people:
I read one-hundred-and-twenty-books in a year.

— This is proof: ——
I documented the entire process online.

— As a result, I learned something counterintuitive: ——
And I learned something valuable:
Execution matters more.

— I took the wrong route because of this failure: ——
I began to read non-stop when two of my startups failed.

— Twist the knife in: ——
I lost all my money.

I wanted an answer:

I wanted to know why this happened to me.

My failures led to more failures. It forced me to take a bad opportunity:

Because my resume looked like chopped liver, I took a job as a low-paid copywriter.

Time went by and I had a counterintuitive aha moment:

Eight months later, I looked up from the pages and realized: I'm still fucken broke.

As a result, I took another direction that involved sacrifices, but held promise:

I stopped reading and took another risk. I took a pay cut from my already low-paid copywriter job to work at a Facebook software startup on contract.

The opportunity provided a tangible benefit, then helped me improve my social standing:

The co-founders took their time to mentor me. Eventually, I worked my way up and became their head of growth.

We had a big win:

We became the first company to live stream on Facebook.

From taking the counterintuitive approach, I gained [X] benefit faster than when I took the common route:

With a month and a half of mentorship, I learned more than I did from reading the one-hundred-and-twenty books.

Here's why:

Why? I jumped into the unknown.

It comes down to these two basic principles:

You won't find the answers to life in a book.
You'll find them living outside your comfort zone.

THEY REJECTED ME
THEN I FOUND PEOPLE WHO DIDN'T

When one of my startups failed, I interviewed at companies across California, including Grammarly and Looker.

I hit a roadblock.

Each company said I could offer value, but I didn't fit the specific role they were hiring for. With no offers, I ran out of savings, moved in with my Dad, then worked my way up to found two companies.

If you believe someone can offer value, don't dismiss them. Give them an opportunity to find a fit.

How?

Put them on contract or start them as an intern.

There's always a place for value.

It's no surprise the one company that did offer me a part-time contract position reaped the rewards—I became their head of growth within several months.

Don't look for people who fit titles.

Look for people who want to solve problems, believe in great work, and share your vision.

— When I had a failure, I looked for a solution: —

When one of my startups failed, I interviewed at companies across California, including Grammarly and Looker.

— I didn't find it: —

I hit a roadblock.

— The opportunities were there, but I couldn't access them. As a result, I lost everything: —

Each company said I could offer value, but I didn't fit the specific role they were hiring for. With no offers, I ran out of savings, moved in with my Dad, then worked my way up to found two companies.

— Don't dismiss people from opportunity: —

If you believe someone can offer value, don't dismiss them.

Give them a chance:

Give them an opportunity to find a fit.

Here's how:

How?
Put them on contract or start them as an intern.

Here's why:

There's always a place for value.

The one person/company who decided to give me opportunity, got the benefits:

It's no surprise the one company that did offer me a part-time contract position reaped the rewards—I became their head of growth within several months.

Don't look for a specific criteria:

Don't look for people who fit titles.

Looking for the characteristics that matter:

Look for people who want to solve problems, believe in great work, and share your vision.

I FOUGHT BIASES
THEN CAME OUT ON TOP

I couldn't land a marketing role at a growing startup in Silicon Valley.

I had four years of startup experience under my belt, including founding a publication that reached an average of 24,000 visitors/day and teaching myself web development.

I recruited 150 writers in three months and published over 300 pieces of content, spent a year copywriting, and another leading marketing at the first company to live stream on Facebook.

The problem: I wasn't in Silicon Valley and didn't have a brand name on my resume.

Startups would rather hire a Stanford graduate with a year of marketing experience at Google than someone who had years of real startup experience and built 6-figure sales funnels from scratch.

I realized the only way to separate myself was to write an entire book about Facebook marketing.

Two-hundred-and-fifty pages later, I landed a role as the head of growth for a fast-growing startup.

That's the problem with Silicon Valley.

They want to see 500 Startups, Y Combinator, Berkeley, and Stanford.

If Silicon Valley wants quality startup talent, then founders and VCs should stop paying attention to vanity brand names and look at metrics.

There are thousands of people who have all the skills in the world, but nobody in Silicon Valley wants to look at them.

Start with the problem:

I couldn't land a marketing role at a growing startup in Silicon Valley.

Why the problem didn't make sense using tangible examples of credibility:

I had four years of startup experience under my belt, including founding a publication that reached an average of 24,000 visitors/day and teaching myself web development.

Dig deeper into why the problem didn't make sense using more tangible examples of credibility:

I recruited 150 writers in three months and published over 300 pieces of content, spent a year copywriting, and another leading marketing at the first company to live stream on Facebook.

Still, I fought bias:

The problem: I wasn't in Silicon Valley and didn't have a brand name on my resume.

Biases included these tangible examples:

Startups would rather hire a Stanford graduate with a year of marketing experience at Google than someone who had years of real startup experience and built 6-figure sales funnels from scratch.

I had to go above and beyond:

I realized the only way to separate myself was to write an entire book about Facebook marketing.

After all of this tangible hard work, I made progress:

Two-hundred-and-fifty pages later, I landed a role as the head of growth for a fast-growing startup.

— This is representative of a bigger problem: —————

That's the problem with Silicon Valley.

— They want vanity metrics: —————

They want to see 500 Startups, Y Combinator, Berkeley, and Stanford.

— Fix this by doing the opposite: —————

If Silicon Valley wants quality startup talent, then founders and VCs should stop paying attention to vanity brand names and look at metrics.

— Why it's important from a bird's eye view: —————

There are thousands of people who have all the skills in the world, but nobody in Silicon Valley wants to look at them.

I DIDN'T GET THE OPPORTUNITY SO I HUSTLED AND MADE IT HAPPEN

I never got an offer from Facebook.

And I've applied multiple times. But that wouldn't stop me from finding a way to make this dream a reality.

In turn, I never expected what would happen next.

Rather than keep applying, I decided to create on their platform.

With my knowledge of Facebook, I built one of the most engaged communities of marketers and founders online.

13,000 members in a Facebook Group.

Facebook loved the community I created, so they gave me a special invite to their Facebook Community Summit in Chicago.

Today, I'm flying out to attend this exclusive conference for the top creators on their platform.

The journey often doesn't make sense because there are so many ways to achieve what we want.

Which is our path?

You can't expect to know.

Our job is to keep chasing because there's always a way.

— Denied an opportunity from a big brand name: —

I never got an offer from Facebook.

— Even though I tried many times. I kept pushing: —

And I've applied multiple times. But that wouldn't stop me from finding a way to make this dream a reality.

— Lead into the next part: —

In turn, I never expected what would happen next.

— I took a more unconventional route: —

Rather than keep applying, I decided to create on their platform.

— It resulted in a large accomplishment: —

With my knowledge of Facebook, I built one of the most engaged communities of marketers and founders online.
13,000 members in a Facebook Group.

This opened the denied opportunity:

Facebook loved the community I created, so they gave me a special invite to their Facebook Community Summit in Chicago.

It's even better than what I wanted in the first place:

Today, I'm flying out to attend this exclusive conference for the top creators on their platform.

I realized the dream is clear, but path is never that way:

The journey often doesn't make sense because there are so many ways to achieve what we want.
Which is our path?
You can't expect to know.

This is why we must do this:

Our job is to keep chasing because there's always a way.

I TOOK THE TRADITIONAL ROUTE
THEN LEFT TO TAKE ACTION

I spent my entire month's salary on a General Assembly course.

I'd learn cutting-edge data analytics skills.

With a strong background in Excel and SQL, I crushed the first half of the course.

Then came project time.

We'd all do the same one based on a fake data set, then give a presentation on it.

I couldn't do it.

The thought of creating the same "fake" project as everyone else killed my creative passion.

So I took a different route.

As the head of growth for an event subscription company, I created an analytics model for event retention using everything I'd learned.

For several weeks, I put every ounce of creative passion in it.

It was an analytics masterpiece.

When it came time to present, everyone was dying of boredom from seeing the same "fake" project over and again.

Then came my turn.

I walked up to the front of the class and said, "I created an analytics model for my company."

Every student perked up.

Why?

I was the only student who solved a real-world problem.

That day several students came up to me and said, "I admire what you did."

I didn't do anything special.

You can always choose to make a real difference.

It's often disguised by the status quo.

It's up to you to break the rules.

That's what entrepreneurs do.

I took a career risk:

I spent my entire month's salary on a General Assembly course.

For this tangible benefit:

I'd learn cutting-edge data analytics skills.

I did exceptionally well:

With a strong background in Excel and SQL, I crushed the first half of the course.

Then the big moment happened where I'd choose a path:

Then came project time.
We'd all do the same one based on a fake data set, then give a presentation on it.

I chose the one everyone else didn't:

I couldn't do it.

It wasn't purpose driven:

The thought of creating the same "fake" project as everyone else killed my creative passion.
So I took a different route.

This route led me to this awesome desired result:

As the head of growth for an event subscription company, I created an analytics model for event retention using everything I'd learned.

It took hard work and was well worth it:

For several weeks, I put every ounce of creative passion in it.
It was an analytics masterpiece.

Here's how I know - people care more about it:

When it came time to present, everyone was dying of boredom from seeing the same "fake" project over and again.
Then came my turn.
I walked up to the front of the class and said, "I created an analytics model for my company."

Tangible example of them caring:

Every student perked up. Why?

In that moment, everyone realized I was right:

I was the only student who solved a real-world problem.
That day several students came up to me and said, "I admire what you did."

I'm not remarkable. I take small actions with a meaningful difference:

I didn't do anything special.
You can always choose to make a real difference.

Look at the bigger picture and don't be afraid:

It's often disguised by the status quo.
It's up to you to break the rules.

Because that's what these respected people do:

That's what entrepreneurs do.

WE DIDN'T GET RESULTS
SO WE CHANGED THE PROCESS

I watched our team spend ten hours on a proposal.

We followed-up with emails and calls.

We heard nothing back.

It's painful to see our team put so much effort into a presentation, then not even get a sentence of feedback.It happens.

We'll listen to the worst feedback to improve. We're excellent problem solvers. That's what makes us exceptional.

We've recently implemented a "why" system.

Whenever someone chooses not to work with us, we ask why.

We tell them it's okay to be brutal.

This nudge took our proposals from beginner to looking sharp in a matter of weeks. It doesn't only work with proposals, but every area of your business.

Never believe you're better than criticism you might receive.

Stay humble.

Ask why.

We invested a lot of time into helping someone:

I watched our team spend ten hours on a proposal.

We tried to keep communication open:

We followed-up with emails and calls.

But we got nothing in return:

We heard nothing back.

It hurts not to receive even one piece of thanks in return:

It's painful to see our team put so much effort into a presentation, then not even get a sentence of feedback. It happens.

To fix this, we always take the higher road. We know that's what works and makes us great:

We'll listen to the worst feedback to improve. We're excellent problem solvers. That's what makes us exceptional.

That's why we have this process to ensure we improve our chances for the future:

We've recently implemented a "why" system.
Whenever someone chooses not to work with us, we ask why.
We tell them it's okay to be brutal.

As a result, we've improved fast:

This nudge took our proposals from beginner to looking sharp in a matter of weeks. It doesn't only work with proposals, but every area of your business.

The learning lesson:

Never believe you're better than criticism you might receive.
Stay humble.
Ask why.

THEY DENIED ME AN OPPORTUNITY SO I ROSE UP

Lyft didn't hire me.

I had two calls with them to help lead their social media efforts.

The first call went well with a junior growth marketer as the interviewer.

"You'll make an impact here."

The second call I had was with a senior growth manager.

"What specifically do you want to do?"

I said, "In the last year, I created one of the largest and most active communities online for founders.

I hosted eighty tech events and racked up 10 million views on Quora.

I've created five social media tools to help automate my workflow.

I'm a problem solver.

Put me anywhere. I'll make a difference."

"We're looking for someone who can fit a specific role like a Facebook marketer."

"I wrote a 300-page technical book on Facebook marketing filled with case studies, but I'm a problem solver, not a Facebook marketer."

He cut the call short.

Not one follow-up.

Four months later, I hit 25 million LinkedIn views then founded two successful companies on track for over 2 million ARR in one year.

This is why companies can't innovate — they don't hire problem solvers.

If you don't fit a specific role, they put you out in the cold.

At Badass Marketers & Founders, we do things differently.

Thank you, Hendry Sukir, for solving enough problems to become one of our first hires.

Problem:

Lyft didn't hire me.

This is what the opportunity looked like:

I had two calls with them to help lead their social media efforts.

At first, I almost had a chance using a tangible instance:

The first call went well with a junior growth marketer as the interviewer.
"You'll make an impact here."

I had one more opportunity:

The second call I had was with a senior growth manager.
"What specifically do you want to do?"

Here's my credibility that over qualifies me using several tangible examples:

I said, "In the last year, I created one of the largest and most active
communities online for founders.
I hosted eighty tech events and racked up 10 million views on Quora.
I've created five social media tools to help automate my workflow.

I don't fit the mold. I'm better than that:

I'm a problem solver.
Put me anywhere. I'll make a difference."

They want someone who can fit the mold in a specific area:

"We're looking for someone who can fit a specific role like a Facebook marketer."

I'm already the best in that area, but don't want to act like a square peg in a round hole:

"I wrote a 300-page technical book on Facebook marketing filled with case studies, but I'm a problem solver, not a Facebook marketer."

They gave me a rude impression:

He cut the call short.

Two times over:

Not one follow-up.

Now I'm even more successful in the area I applied to help in:

Four months later, I hit 25 million LinkedIn views then founded two successful companies on track for over 2 million ARR in one year.

—— This represents a culture problem that hurts them: ——

This is why companies can't innovate - they don't hire problem solvers.

—— But also hurts the people like me: ——

If you don't fit a specific role, they put you out in the cold.

—— That's why I/we do things differently: ——

At Badass Marketers & Founders, we do things differently.

—— And the best we can do is the opposite with a thank- ——
you example:

Thank you, Hendry Sukir, for solving enough problems to become one of our first hires.

I DIDN'T GET AN OPPORTUNITY SO I GAVE SOMEONE ELSE ONE

When one of my startups failed, I became desperate.

I ran out of cash and began walking into companies unannounced applying for entry-level writing positions.

It hurt.

Each company said I could offer value, but didn't hire me.

I took a bottom of the barrel copywriting job convinced I would crawl out.

I worked as a copywriter under a marketing manager who ignored me, and a boss who'd throw her feet up on my desk when talking to me.

As soon as I saved up enough money to escape, I joined a Facebook software startup to hone my technical writing skills.

Now I write many of the most-viewed technical how-to posts on the web.

If you believe someone can offer value, don't shut the door on them.

And don't start them with a small task.

Give them a chance to find their task.

Why?

Excellent problem solvers seek where they add the most value.

For me—that's writing.

Today, we hired a new employee for **BAMF** Media.

She reminded me of myself.

Yesterday, she knocked on our door without a scheduled interview.

True hustle.

The problem: she had visa issues and was overqualified.

She had three days to get hired or she'd be deported.

We decided to move forward for one reason:

I promised myself I'd be better than my past experiences.

Today, I had the chance to prove it.

┌─── **Something bad happened and left me vulnerable:** ───┐

When one of my startups failed, I became desperate.

I lost this valuable asset and desperately tried out for these lower opportunities:

I ran out of cash and began walking into companies unannounced applying for entry-level writing positions.
It hurt.

They didn't even want me:

Each company said I could offer value, but didn't hire me.

I took the only opportunity I could find:

I took a bottom of the barrel copywriting job convinced I would crawl out.

It was awful for these tangible reasons:

I worked as a copywriter under a marketing manager who ignored me, and a boss who'd throw her feet up on my desk when talking to me.

I left as soon as I could for a new opportunity:

As soon as I saved up enough money to escape, I joined a Facebook software startup to hone my technical writing skills.

—— That'd lead to this awesome tangible result: ——

Now I write many of the most-viewed technical how-to posts on the web.

—— Never close an opportunity because someone is ——
different:

If you believe someone can offer value, don't shut the door on them. And don't start them with a small task.

—— Give them a chance to find their fit: ——

Give them a chance to find their task. Why?

—— Because the right people will find it: ——

Excellent problem solvers seek where they add the most value.

—— My unique skill is X: ——

For me—that's writing.

Today someone wanted to partner/work with/for me and they reminded me of myself:

Today, we hired a new employee for BAMF Media.
She reminded me of myself.'

Tangible example of how:

Yesterday, she knocked on our door without a scheduled interview.
True hustle.

Her unique problem:

The problem: she had visa issues and was overqualified.
She had three days to get hired or she'd be deported.

We still moved forward because it's similar to what I went through:

We decided to move forward for one reason:
I promised myself I'd be better than my past experiences.
Today, I had the chance to prove it.

DON'T PIGGYBACK
OFF THE BACK OF OTHERS

Yesterday, I was riding in an Uber, and the driver had just finished working an entire month. No breaks.

He's one of those people who you remember because he's self-made and has a world of ambition.

But here he was working an insane number of hours.

All for what?

To pay his daughter's student loans.

She went to an expensive private college to study design. Without many job prospects, she went back and started her masters.

He hesitated when mentioning the student loans.

He could barely justify it.

"Why design? I understand she loves it. But it's hard, you know? We put in all this work. Why not a doctor?"

Many students don't realize the pain they give their parents.

We have access to Udemy, trade schools, YouTube, Quora, Stack Overflow, Google, and more.

Do we really need many of these degrees?

College is one option.

And not the best one if it requires students to step on their parent's back when they have dreams of their own.

Maybe their parents want to start a new company, write a book or volunteer around the community.

Don't they deserve that?

Be resourceful.

Be kind.

Especially to parents.

And rather than take — students should work a job that enables them to pay for college.

Help them understand they need to work for what they want.

Common and intimate setting where I met someone with a problem:

Yesterday, I was riding in an Uber, and the driver had just finished working an entire month. No breaks.

They were a good person:

He's one of those people who you remember because he's self-made and has a world of ambition.

But in this awful situation:

But here he was working an insane number of hours.
All for what?

For someone they loved:

To pay his daughter's student loans.

Even though that person made the wrong decisions:

She went to an expensive private college to study design. Without many job prospects, she went back and started her masters.

It hurts them:

He hesitated when mentioning the student loans.
He could barely justify it.

Tangible conversation expressing pain:

"Why design? I understand she loves it. But it's hard, you know? We put in all this work. Why not a doctor?"

These loved ones don't realize the pain they cause:

Many students don't realize the pain they give their parents.

They can do these tangible things instead:

We have access to Udemy, trade schools, YouTube, Quora, Stack Overflow, Google, and more.

We need to ask this question:

Do we really need many of these degrees?

Because of this:

College is one option.

This is not the best way to do it:

And not the best one if it requires students to step on their parent's back when they have dreams of their own.

Remember their dreams:

Maybe their parents want to start a new company, write a book or volunteer around the community.

They deserve it:

Don't they deserve that?
Be resourceful.
Be kind.
Especially to parents.

Do this next time to show them the right way:

And rather than take — students should work a job that enables them to pay for college.
Help them understand they need to work for what they want.

OVERCAME BIASES THAT WE NEED TO FIX

What's your chip on your shoulder?

Would you imagine that a little over a year ago, I couldn't land a marketing role at a growing startup in Silicon Valley?

I had four years of startup experience under my belt, including founding a publication that reached an average of 24,000 visitors/day and teaching myself web development.

I recruited 150 writers in three months and published over 300 pieces of content, spent a year copywriting, and another leading marketing at the first company to live stream on Facebook.

The problem: I wasn't in Silicon Valley and didn't have a brand name on my resume.

Startups would rather hire the graduate from Stanford with a year of marketing experience at Google than someone who had years of real startup experience and built 6-figure sales funnels from scratch.

All because I lived in another city, went to a state school, and didn't work for a well-known corporate company.

At some point, I realized the only way to separate myself was to write an entire book about Facebook marketing.

Two-hundred-and-fifty pages later, I landed a role as the head of growth for a fast-growing startup.

That's the problem with Silicon Valley.

Nobody cares about you if you don't have a brand name on your resume.

Doesn't matter what you've done.

They want to see 500 Startups, Y Combinator, Berkeley, and Stanford.

If Silicon Valley really wants to take care of their diversity problems, then maybe many of the founders and VCs should stop paying attention to vanity brand names and look at metrics.

No wonder when I came to Silicon Valley they didn't have a single community that gave startup founders cutting-edge tactics.

In the tech mecca of the world, they could care less.

Accelerators rather take your equity and give you a mentor who's never been a founder or created traction from scratch.

That's my chip.

It's what drives me every day.

They're thousands of people who have all the skills in the world, but nobody in Silicon Valley wants to look at them.

Start with a statement that implies you're about to rant:

What's your chip on your shoulder?

You know my credibility, but other people used to doubt me:

Would you imagine that a little over a year ago, I couldn't land a marketing role at a growing startup in Silicon Valley?

In case you don't know me, here's my credibility backed by hard numbers:

I had four years of startup experience under my belt, including founding a publication that reached an average of 24,000 visitors/day and teaching myself web development.

I recruited 150 writers in three months and published over 300 pieces of content, spent a year copywriting, and another leading marketing at the first company to live stream on Facebook.

None of it matters because of this:

The problem: I wasn't in Silicon Valley and didn't have a brand name on my resume.

Make it tangible with an example:

Startups would rather hire the graduate from Stanford with a year of marketing experience at Google than someone who had years of real startup experience and built 6-figure sales funnels from scratch.

All because of a petty pre-conceived notion:

All because I lived in another city, went to a state school, and didn't work for a well-known corporate company.

I needed to overcome this problem. There was only one way:

At some point, I realized the only way to separate myself was to write an entire book about Facebook marketing.

As a result of brutally hard work, I accomplished my goal:

Two-hundred-and-fifty pages later, I landed a role as the head of growth for a fast-growing startup.

There's a bigger problem at hand:

That's the problem with Silicon Valley.
Nobody cares about you if you don't have a brand name on your resume.

Knife twisting:

Doesn't matter what you've done.
They want to see 500 Startups, Y Combinator, Berkeley, and Stanford.

To fix this problem:

If Silicon Valley really wants to take care of their diversity problems, then maybe many of the founders and VCs should stop paying attention to vanity brand names and look at metrics.

No surprise there's also this HUGE related problem:

No wonder when I came to Silicon Valley they didn't have a single community that gave startup founders cutting-edge tactics.

Can you believe it?

In the tech mecca of the world, they could care less.

Knife twisting:

Accelerators rather take your equity and give you a mentor who's never been a founder or created traction from scratch.

Tie it back:

That's my chip.
It's what drives me every day.

It's not about me, it's about everyone who needs our help:

They're thousands of people who have all the skills in the world, but nobody in Silicon Valley wants to look at them.

DON'T GIVE ADVICE

I can't stand people who give career advice on what jobs people should do.

My parents have no idea what I do.

My job didn't even exist a couple of years ago.

With today's learning advancements, we're creating the next generation of opportunities.

We need to allow students to chase more creative routes.

Routes that didn't exist when we grew up.

Let them learn data science, programming, or engineering at an earlier age.

Not every student needs to sit through a math class where the teacher refuses to let them use calculators.

Or pulls them off of their phone because "they're not reading" from a book.

We're in a tech-driven world.

I can't tell a student what career to choose.

I don't even know what careers will be available once they get into the workforce in four years or even six months.

All I can do is encourage the right mindset while making connections where need be — whether investors or mentors.

Your path is not theirs.

It's to hand these young pioneers a light when everything goes dark.

Don't take advice from people:

I can't stand people who give career advice on what jobs people should do.

Traditional people don't understand:

My parents have no idea what I do.

I can't blame them:

My job didn't even exist a couple of years ago.

The world is changing too fast to give advice:

With today's learning advancements, we're creating the next generation of opportunities. We need to allow students to chase more creative routes. Routes that didn't exist when we grew up.

We need people to learn these cutting-edge things:

Let them learn data science, programming, or engineering at an earlier age.

They should no longer go through these old traditional routes:

Not every student needs to sit through a math class where the teacher refuses to let them use calculators.
Or pulls them off of their phone because "they're not reading" from a book.

This is the world today:

We're in a tech-driven world.

I can't even give advice:

I can't tell a student what career to choose.

Because I can't predict it:

I don't even know what careers will be available once they get into the workforce in four years or even six months.

Here's how I can help people think differently:

All I can do is encourage the right mindset while making connections where need be - whether investors or mentors.

Don't tell people to walk in your shoes:

Your path is not theirs.

Help them find their own path:

It's to hand these young pioneers a light when everything goes dark.

MY BIGGEST MISTAKE

I hit my lowest point.

Not when I lost $500,000 of investor money.

Not when I got kicked out of a company.

It's when I blamed my own faults on my co-founder.

We recruited 150 writers, and we were driving 24,000 visitors every day to our online publication. Everything seemed perfect.

And I let my ego get the best of me.

I turned down fantastic job offers telling hiring managers we were building a hundred million dollar company.

Lies.

Deep down I knew it was all falling apart.

A year later, it did.

We had no revenue.

New to online marketing and entrepreneurship, we were still figuring out the basics to product/market fit and monetization.

As a bootstrapped startup, we didn't have the runway to figure it out.

We needed answers.

I yelled at my co-founder, blaming him for not finding a way to make our company money. He didn't fight back.

He took the blame.

We pivoted.

It failed.

I fired all 150 writers.

Then people on the managerial team.

As the co-founder and CEO, I didn't realized it was my fault.

I didn't have the self-awareness to lose my ego. Instead, I lost my best friend and co-founder.

We're friends now, but I totally screwed up.

Today, I thank my co-founder every day.

It takes a lot of courage to remind yourself that you're never perfect.

At the bottom:

I hit my lowest point.

It wasn't these bad, tangible things:

Not when I lost $500,000 of investor money.
Not when I got kicked out of a company.

It's when this bad tangible thing happened:

It's when I blamed my own faults on my co-founder.

I had this great tangible accomplishment:

We recruited 150 writers, and we were driving 24,000 visitors every day to our online publication. *Everything seemed perfect.*

But then everything went downhill:

And I let my ego get the best of me.

I even did this dumb thing:

I turned down fantastic job offers telling hiring managers we were building a hundred million dollar company. Lies.

I knew it was falling apart:

Deep down I knew it was all falling apart.
A year later, it did.

Here's why:

We had no revenue.
New to online marketing and entrepreneurship, we were still figuring out the basics to product/market fit and monetization.

And we made these mistakes at the worst time:

As a bootstrapped startup, we didn't have the runway to figure it out.
We needed answers.

I couldn't see that it was my fault:

I yelled at my co-founder, blaming him for not finding a way to make our company money. He didn't fight back.
He took the blame.

Then it all fell apart (escalate the failure):

We pivoted.
It failed.
I fired all 150 writers.
Then people on the managerial team.

But it was all my fault:

As the co-founder and CEO, I didn't realized it was my fault.

Here's why:

I didn't have the self-awareness to lose my ego. Instead, I lost my best friend and co-founder.

It's fine now, but I fucked up:

We're friends now, but I totally screwed up.

─ Now I don't take it for granted: ────────────

Today, I thank my co-founder every day.

─ Inspirational line of why it's okay to be vulnerable: ───

It takes a lot of courage to remind yourself that you're never perfect.

ATTACKED FOR A UNIQUE CULTURE

People attacked me.

Hundreds of negative comments because of our company culture.

We remove soda from our workplace and encourage people to work out.

As the co-founder, I built a health conscious company.

Does everyone fit in with our culture? No.

We don't need everyone.

We need people who we want to surround ourselves with.

Most companies don't care at all about their employees' health.

To keep employees longer, they go to the other end of the spectrum.

More bean bags.

More candy jars.

More happy hours.

This attitude gets people addicted to your culture for the wrong reasons.

My culture doesn't have to be yours.

Nor do I force people to accept it.

People have a right to choose where they want to work.

If we scare the majority of our applicants away, then that's fine.

We're for the few.

That's what makes us exceptional.

And we'll do whatever we can to keep it that way.

┌─ **They came after me:** ────────────────────

People attacked me.

├─ **Doing these negative things:** ────────────

Hundreds of negative comments because of our company culture.

├─ **Because of this reason:** ────────────────

We remove soda from our workplace and encourage people to work out.

└──

I chose this route:

As the co-founder, I built a health conscious company.

It's not for everyone:

Does everyone fit in with our culture? No.

That's fine:

We don't need everyone.

We associate with people we like:

We need people who we want to surround ourselves with.

Few do what we do:

Most companies don't care at all about their employees' health.

Here's what they do wrong with these tangible examples:

To keep employees longer, they go to the other end of the spectrum.
More bean bags.
More candy jars.
More happy hours.

It leads to this negative outcome:

This attitude gets people addicted to your culture for the wrong reasons.

Let people be unique:

My culture doesn't have to be yours.

I let people choose:

Nor do I force people to accept it.
People have a right to choose where they want to work.

We don't care if we end up with only a few:

If we scare the majority of our applicants away, then that's fine. We're for the few.

That's what makes us great:

That's what makes us exceptional.

We'll keep it that way:

And we'll do whatever we can to keep it that way.

SHORT-TERM SACRIFICE FOR BIG GAINS

We fired our first employee on his first day.

This was week one of our startup.

Hiring is brutal for an early-stage company looking to scale fast.

We're not perfect.

Far from it.

As the CEO, I spent five percent of my time hiring.

This led to rushed decisions and bringing on candidates with red flags.

We lost hundreds of hours and it almost suffocated our business.

This week we hired three new employees.

A senior growth strategist.

A copywriter.

A designer.

All rockstars.

We searched through thousands of candidates to find them.

To do this, I delegated half of my tasks.

The problem?

These tasks had an immediate effect on revenue. We had to lose money to make money.

I had to take the risk.

Without the right employees, you'll never scale.

Your company will remain you and your co-founder.

Whenever I question my investment in hiring, I always remember a great vision without great people is irrelevant.

We made a tough business decision:

We fired our first employee on his first day.

In a rough time:

This was week one of our startup.

It's not easy when you're in our position:

Hiring is brutal for an early-stage company looking to scale fast.

── It's not rainbows and sunshine: ──────────

We're not perfect. Far from it.

── This is what I did wrong: ──────────

As the CEO, I spent five percent of my time hiring.

── This led to these tangible problems: ──────────

This led to rushed decisions and bringing on candidates with red flags.
We lost hundreds of hours and it almost suffocated our business.

── Then we made progress: ──────────

This week we hired three new employees. A senior growth strategist.
A copywriter. A designer. All rockstars.

── It happened because we did the opposite: ──────────

We searched through thousands of candidates to find them.
To do this, I delegated half of my tasks.

At first, we took a hit in a counterintuitive way:

The problem? These tasks had an immediate effect on revenue. We had to lose money to make money. I had to take the risk.

It didn't matter, we knew it would lead to a positive outcome:

Without the right employees, you'll never scale.

If you don't, then you'll never grow:

Your company will remain you and your co-founder.

Inspirational quote about building a foundation:

Whenever I question my investment in hiring, I always remember a great vision without great people is irrelevant.

STARTED FROM THE BOTTOM
FOCUS ON THE SMALL THINGS

Jinny (Hyojin) Oh

My very first client paid me $5/hr (I wrote 3 articles for $30 *total*).

I wasn't upset, but rather ecstatic.

This was exactly 3 years ago. At this point in my life, I held two Master's degrees and could've easily had a 6-figure job. Instead, I was excited over $5/hr, which barely paid for a gallon of gas in LA; however, it was the thought that this was the 'start' of endless possibilities that excited me.

Going from 0 to 1 is the hardest. If I can get one client, what's to stop me from getting 2, or 3 or even 10?

After my first project with this client, he wrote a paragraph long review of how I was the *best* freelancer he's ever hired. Since that day, I've worked with over 200 clients who've all added value to my credibility.

Today, I'm no longer a one-girl operation, but part of a 15-person team called Wander Agency. Our prices increased 3000% since the day I started and we make more revenue in one month than I did my whole first year.

It's important to know your worth, but you also have to start somewhere small.

All the 'big dream' ideas I had failed because I'd bite off more than I could chew. Wander, however, has grown month after month because of the foundations I built.

Rome wasn't built in a day. Neither should your business.

I started at the lowest of positions:

*My very first client paid me $5/hr (I wrote 3 articles for $30 **total**).*

It was a sign of progress:

I wasn't upset, but rather ecstatic.

This happened at this point in my life when I had so much credibility:

This was exactly 3 years ago. At this point in my life, I held two Master's degrees and could've easily had a 6-figure job.

But I chose this route instead because it aligned with my dreams:

Instead, I was excited over $5/hr, which barely paid for a gallon of gas in LA; however, it was the thought that this was the 'start' of endless possibilities that excited me.

It's hard to start, but then you have momentum:

Going from 0 to 1 is the hardest. If I can get one client, what's to stop me from getting 2, or 3 or even 10?

Step one gave me the credibility I needed:

*After my first project with this client, he wrote a paragraph long review of how I was the **best** freelancer he's ever hired. Since that day, I've worked with over 200 clients who've all added value to my credibility.*

Today, we have a lot of credibility with a big, positive outlook:

Today, I'm no longer a one-girl operation, but part of a 15-person team called Wander Agency. Our prices increased 3000% since the day I started and we make more revenue in one month than I did my whole first year.

Know what you can be, but know it takes the little things:

It's important to know your worth, but you also have to start somewhere small.

— Don't reach for the stars. Start by building a rocket —
knowing one day you'll get there:

All the 'big dream' ideas I had failed because I'd bite off more than I could chew. Wander, however, has grown month after month because of the foundations I built.

— Takes time—inspirational quote: ————————————

Rome wasn't built in a day. Neither should your business.

TRADITIONAL JOB PROBLEMS

I met a nice banker who's been working for Wells Fargo for the last several years.

As I was filing paperwork with him, he told me his plan to start his own company that helps local businesses with social media.

He said he's been working on his business plan for two and a half years.

The chances are that this person will never launch their business.

They will continue working their 9-5 job.

Today, you can get validation for your product or service in less than a week, and for some of us, it's less than a day.

Industries are changing so fast that making business plans for the next six months won't do you much good. And it may just chain your ankles around a corporate desk chair for the rest of your life.

The banker explained how his MBA experience helped him make his business plan. Your MBA teaches you to plan, plan, and plan some more.

MBAs are outdated.

Ten years ago, you couldn't get validation for your product or service as fast as you can now.

Many people don't pay enough attention to technological advancements; as a result, they spend an enormous amount of money on an outdated education.

There's no reason to wait to become an entrepreneur.

Creating value for others has never been as easy.

Life is too short to plan everything.

Stop waiting.

─ I met a person who works a traditional job: ─

I met a nice banker who's been working for Wells Fargo for the last several years.

─ They told me about their dreams: ─

As I was filing paperwork with him, he told me his plan to start his own company that helps local businesses with social media.

─ How they've been preparing over and again: ─

He said he's been working on his business plan for two and a half years.

The problem:

The chances are that this person will never launch their business.

Life for them won't change:

They will continue working their 9-5 job.

Stop waiting. Take action:

Today, you can get validation for your product or service in less than a week, and for some of us, it's less than a day.

Business plans are of the past — it will make you complacent:

Industries are changing so fast that making business plans for the next six months won't do you much good. And it may just chain your ankles around a corporate desk chair for the rest of your life.

The person paid these people to help planning:

The banker explained how his MBA experience helped him make his business plan. Your MBA teaches you to plan, plan, and plan some more.
MBAs are outdated.

Times are different:

Ten years ago, you couldn't get validation for your product or service as fast as you can now.

If you don't keep up, you'll get left behind:

Many people don't pay enough attention to technological advancements; as a result, they spend an enormous amount of money on an outdated education.

If you're an entrepreneur, the time is always now:

There's no reason to wait to become an entrepreneur.

Inspirational lines about taking action:

Creating value for others has never been as easy.
Life is too short to plan everything.
Stop waiting.

ADVICE I TOOK TO HELP ME RISE ABOVE FAILURE

My boss left me after day one.

Several weeks later, I received an email — "We're letting you go."

She disappeared to raise funding, then never got it.

I didn't understand.

My college roommate was the first employee at a growing startup.

After three months, he was making close to $200K annually.

This was my first impression of startup life.

And here I was getting fired from an unpaid startup internship.

My roommate's success was the best thing to ever happen to me.

It gave me the courage to work for four more failed startups.

Because I saw it was possible.

Rather than scream that life wasn't fair, I took it as a positive sign.

I asked what made him successful.

He replied, "I have the mentality of a rock climber. I don't pay attention to politics or TV. I focus on what I can control. The three feet around me."

Since that conversation, I dialed in my focus.

The next year and a half, I read close to 200 books about business.

Then published over 1000 articles.

Five years later, I've stepped into similar shoes as my roommate. I'm the co-founder of one of the fastest growing agencies, **BAMF** Media.

If you want something bad enough - stop craving control for what's out of reach.

Think like a rock climber.

You'll feel confident.

You'll feel empowered.

I had a big negative life change:

My boss left me after day one.

Then it got worse:

Several weeks later, I received an email - "We're letting you go."

— Why it happened: —————————————————

She disappeared to raise funding, then never got it.

— I didn't get it: ——————————————————

I didn't understand.

— Because I saw people have positive life changes under — similar circumstances:

My college roommate was the first employee at a growing startup.

— With this tangible example: ————————————

After three months, he was making close to $200K annually.

— Here's why I believed it: —————————————

This was my first impression of startup life.

— But I was experiencing the opposite: ———

And here I was getting fired from an unpaid startup internship.

— It didn't matter because it gave me hope: ———

My roommate's success was the best thing to ever happen to me.

— To overcome these tangible obstacles: ———

It gave me the courage to work for four more failed startups.
Because I saw it was possible.

— I saw the positive in the negative: ———

Rather than scream that life wasn't fair, I took it as a positive sign.

— So asked them why they experience the positive: ———

I asked what made him successful.

The reply (learning lesson):

He replied, "I have the mentality of a rock climber. I don't pay attention to politics or TV. I focus on what I can control. The three feet around me."

I took the feedback and went all in:

Since that conversation, I dialed in my focus.

With these tangible actions:

The next year and a half, I read close to 200 books about business. Then published over 1000 articles.

As a result, now I have this positive experience:

Five years later, I've stepped into similar shoes as my roommate. I'm the co-founder of one of the fastest growing agencies, BAMF Media.

Summarize the learning lesson:

If you want something bad enough - stop craving control for what's out of reach. Think like a rock climber.

Inspirational lines:

You'll feel confident. You'll feel empowered.

DON'T DEFINE YOURSELF
BY YOUR MISTAKES

My employee made a mistake.

It could've cost us a potential client.

I laughed about it.

Rather than scold him, I explained that he's more valuable now after learning from his mistake.

If he makes a $50,000 mistake, then that's a $50,000 learning lesson I don't have to pay for again.

I said, "Don't define yourself on what you've done. Define yourself on where you're headed."

If I defined myself as a dishwasher, I would've never stepped into digital marketing.

As a failed founder?

I would've never founded a successful company.

As a poor fiction writer?

I would've never had millions of people read my work.

You are not your mistakes.

You are everything you're aiming to become.

Because if you want it bad enough, it will happen.

And I know he does.

— A person I cared for made a mistake: ————————

My employee made a mistake.

— It could've led to a bad outcome: ————————

It could've cost us a potential client.

— I looked at it as a blessing: ————————

I laughed about it.

— I gave them the benefit of the doubt: ————————

Rather than scold him, I explained that he's more valuable now after learning from his mistake.

— Because, at the end of the day, you learn from ———— mistakes:

If he makes a $50,000 mistake, then that's a $50,000 learning lesson I don't have to pay for again.

— I told them that mistakes don't define you (with — inspirational line):

I said, "Don't define yourself on what you've done. Define yourself on where you're headed."

— Because I'd never be here if I thought that way with — these three tangible examples:

If I defined myself as a dishwasher, I would've never stepped into digital marketing.
As a failed founder?
I would've never founded a successful company.
As a poor fiction writer?
I would've never had millions of people read my work.

— Don't define yourself by mistakes: —

You are not your mistakes.

— Define yourself by where you're headed: —

You are everything you're aiming to become.

Believe it — and it will happen:

Because if you want it bad enough, it will happen.
And I know he does.

BAD CULTURE MOVE
SO I MOVED ON & THEY LOST EVERYTHING

They posted my job online.

I was getting fired.

And I found out in the worst way.

When my manager greeted me with a smile, I couldn't even look at him.

He betrayed me.

I wasn't ready for the conversation.

So I didn't mention it.

Instead, I broke down and told all my coworkers at lunch time.

"They're letting me go. I saw my job posted online."

One employee spoke up.

"That's how the last two people in your position found out."

In a brief second, every employee lost faith in management.

It destroyed their culture.

The next few days, I did zero work.

I applied to hundreds of jobs.

I got three interviews.

At the end of the week, I got an email from my CEO.

"Let's find a time to talk."

I walked into her office ready to quit.

She said, "We understand you saw your job posted online. To be upfront, we are looking for someone else."

I replied, "I won't wait here. It's best I go."

I left never wanting to hear the company's name again.

It doesn't matter how talented your employees are.

It doesn't matter how much funding you secure.

You need a transparent culture.

No matter how small the details.

Because companies are not built on the foundation of revenue.

They're built on the foundation of mutual respect.

And that starts with people.

I found out about a negative change in my future:

They posted my job online.

— It would lead to this negative outcome: —

I was getting fired.

— This was the worst way for things to happen: —

And I found out in the worst way.

— So when they tried to pretend like it didn't happen, it —
hurt me:

When my manager greeted me with a smile, I couldn't even look at him.
He betrayed me.
I wasn't ready for the conversation.
So I didn't mention it.

— I told everyone about the situation who mattered: —

Instead, I broke down and told all my coworkers at lunch time.
"They're letting me go. I saw my job posted online."
One employee spoke up.

— Then I found out it's worse than I thought: —

"That's how the last two people in your position found out."

— Everyone tied to the situation saw the problem: —

In a brief second, every employee lost faith in management.

— It resulted in this negative effect for management: —

It destroyed their culture.

— Rather than continue, I prepared, took action, got — results:

The next few days, I did zero work.
I applied to hundreds of jobs.
I got three interviews.

— Then the fateful day happened: —

At the end of the week, I got an email from my CEO.
"Let's find a time to talk."
I walked into her office ready to quit.

— They mentioned they knew I saw what happened: —

She said, "We understand you saw your job posted online. To be upfront, we are looking for someone else."

─ I made the process faster: ────────────

I replied, "I won't wait here. It's best I go."

─ I don't care for the company anymore: ───────

I left never wanting to hear the company's name again.

─ Even if they have these tangible benefits: ─────

It doesn't matter how talented your employees are.
It doesn't matter how much funding you secure.

─ They need to operate better: ───────────

You need a transparent culture.
No matter how small the details.

─ It comes down to people: ──────────────

Because companies are not built on the foundation of revenue.
They're built on the foundation of mutual respect.
And that starts with people.

LOVED ONES OVER WORK

AARON AGIUS

My five year old son woke me up at near 5am one morning telling me he had a problem in the living room and needed my help now.

I'm never thrilled about being up at that time of day and to be told he had a problem meant I was already angry by the time I got downstairs.

When I got downstairs he was sitting at his small table working on a drawing.

I asked him, rather abruptly "What's the problem??"

He responded "We don't get to draw together much anymore because you're away for work and I'm trying to draw a picture of me and you at the park and I keep going outside the lines — can you help?".

Instant paradigm shift.

I went from tired and cranky, to remorseful and emotional in an instant.

I travel a lot for work as we have clients globally and my wife and I both work hard to support the family financially.

My son taught me a valuable lesson that day.

You can work your hands to the bone, getting all sorts of business accolades, buying new clothes and other fancy material things, but in the end it's quite simple.

What kids need most is time, not material things.

Family first always.

Someone I cared about interrupted me and told me they needed help:

My five year old son woke me up at near 5am one morning telling me he had a problem in the living room and needed my help now.

I was upset about the interruption:

I'm never thrilled about being up at that time of day and to be told he had a problem meant I was already angry by the time I got downstairs.

Then I saw them:

When I got downstairs he was sitting at his small table working on a drawing.

I asked about the problem:

I asked him, rather abruptly "What's the problem??"

They responded it's about the time we spend together:

He responded "We don't get to draw together much anymore because you're away for work and I'm trying to draw a picture of me and you at the park and I keep going outside the lines - can you help?".
Instant paradigm shift.

I felt horrible about it:

I went from tired and cranky, to remorseful and emotional in an instant.

Sometimes I forget about the people who mean the most to me:

I travel a lot for work as we have clients globally and my wife and I both work hard to support the family financially.

They taught me a valuable lesson:

My son taught me a valuable lesson that day.

Work is not that important:

You can work your hands to the bone, getting all sorts of business accolades, buying new clothes and other fancy material things, but in the end it's quite simple.

It's the experience with those who matter the most that is:

What kids need most is time, not material things.
Family first always.

HELP SOMEONE OUT IN NEED BY CHANCE

"I don't know what I'm going to do."

I overheard the woman sitting next to me in the coffee shop burst into tears.

I personally wasn't having a great day, but I listened as she told her friend she was on her way back from an interview.

"I really needed that job," she cried.

I overheard that she was a mother of young children and needed flexibility that most companies weren't willing to provide.

She'd been searching for months and kept coming up empty.

I couldn't help but notice how committed this lady was and admired how much she wanted to get back to work.

Her friend left first and as she was getting up to leave something made me lean over and introduce myself.

I asked what line of work she was in.

"I used to do Marketing".

As I introduced myself as the CEO of a global marketing agency, her face turned to shock.

We weren't hiring at the time, but I called a friend who hired her and she started working within a week.

I couldn't get over the timing that created the situation.

But that's just how the world works sometimes.

It was a reminder to me to stay open and aware of other people's lives and not just my own.

You never know who's around you who could change your life.

Reach out and try to help everyone you meet. The connections you make will astound you.

I overheard someone with a problem:

"I don't know what I'm going to do."
I overheard the woman sitting next to me in the coffee shop burst into tears.

I wasn't having a good day, but I overhead them that they were in dire need:

I personally wasn't having a great day, but I listened as she told her friend she was on her way back from an interview. "I really needed that job," she cried.

They weren't in the best position:

I overheard that she was a mother of young children and needed flexibility that most companies weren't willing to provide.

— After months of trying, they'd lost everything: —

She'd been searching for months and kept coming up empty.

— They were committed and I admired that: —

I couldn't help but notice how committed this lady was and admired how much she wanted to get back to work.

— After the phone call/talk, they were about to leave so — I introduced myself:

Her friend left first and as she was getting up to leave something made me lean over and introduce myself.

— I asked them about themselves: —

I asked what line of work she was in. "I used to do Marketing".

— I then introduced myself as someone who could help: —

As i introduced myself as the CEO of a global marketing agency, her face turned to shock.

We weren't in the position to give an opportunity, but I gave them a hand that did:

We weren't hiring at the time, but I called a friend who hired her and she started working within a week.

The timing was perfect:

I couldn't get over the timing that created the situation.

Sometimes life works out that way:

But that's just how the world works sometimes.

It's a reminder to pay attention to other people's lives:

It was a reminder to me to stay open and aware of other people's lives and not just my own.

Because life is full of gifts — we just need to see them:

You never know who's around you who could change your life.

Inspirational note:

Reach out and try to help everyone you meet. The connections you make will astound you.

PEOPLE YOU CARE ABOUT
BEFORE WORK

— Aaron Agius

It's brutal.

Waking up at 2am to put your kids back to sleep.

Then getting back up at 6am to go to work.

I did it because it makes me a great father.

As a young parent running a company, it's hard to find the balance.

You want to be the best you can for your kids, but you want the best business success so your employees can spend time with theirs.

You have to champion them all.

The hardest part as an entrepreneur — it's never enough.

With kids, the problem grows because you have less money, focus, and sleep. You feel like you have to put more time into work — but you can't.

I focus as much as I can to ensure I can come home by dinner time every night with my kids. A lot of businessmen I know only care about making this happen a couple of days a week at best.

Kids deserve better.

I remember years ago, with one of our first international prospects for our agency.

We'd put weeks into the proposal and negotiations. Then they told me that they could only do weekly meetings after 7 p.m.

I said "no."

And lost the client.

I'd be lying to say I didn't think about flipping my schedule.

The problem: That's the same time when I'm home to play with my kids.

And seeing my kids smile when I open the front door means the world to me.

It reminds me of why I became a father.

Vague pain statement:

It's brutal.

I work hard with these tangible examples:

Waking up at 2am to put your kids back to sleep.
Then getting back up at 6am to go to work.

But it makes me a great person:

I did it because it makes me a great father.

The balance is hard:

As a young parent running a company, it's hard to find the balance.

I need to be there for the people I care about, but also other people who depend on me:

You want to be the best you can for your kids, but you want the best business success so your employees can spend time with theirs.

You need to own it all:

You have to champion them all.

It's never enough:

The hardest part as an entrepreneur — it's never enough.

It will only get harder:

With kids, the problem grows because you have less money, focus, and sleep. You feel like you have to put more time into work - but you can't.

I try to be there for the ones I care about. Not everyone does this:

I focus as much as I can to ensure I can come home by dinner time every night with my kids. A lot of businessmen I know only care about making this happen a couple of days a week at best.

They deserve more:

Kids deserve better.

There was a time when I almost messed up:

I remember years ago, with one of our first international prospects for our agency.

For this opportunity:

We'd put weeks into the proposal and negotiations. Then they told me that they could only do weekly meetings after 7 p.m.

But I didn't:

I said "no."

I lost the opportunity:

And lost the client.

I did think about it:

I'd be lying to say I didn't think about flipping my schedule.

But it would cut into the time I spend caring:

The problem: That's the same time when I'm home to play with my kids.

I knew it would never replace this tangible moment of pure joy:

And seeing my kids smile when I open the front door means the world to me.

It reminds me of why I chose this path:

It reminds me of why I became a father.

FINDING BALANCE WHEN CARING BEFORE OTHERS & WORK

It's rough.

Every morning I hit the gym at 4:30 am.

Then get to the office by 7 a.m. to write for two hours.

I do it because it makes me a better employer.

As a young entrepreneur running a company, it's hard to find balance.

You want to be at the top of your game for your employees, but you don't want to sacrifice your health.

You have to do it all.

And as a founder — you're never satisfied.

You want to put more into work, but you can't.

There will always be more tasks.

I ensure to come home with an hour to talk to family and friends.

But this doesn't always happen.

Back when we only had four people on the team, we once signed several clients in a day for **BAMF** Media.

For a week, I didn't get any sleep and missed every workout.

It took me an entire month to get back into my routine.

I vowed I would never do this again.

Today, I set better expectations for my clients.

Rather than say "today," I'll say "two weeks."

I'd be lying if I stated that I no longer get pressured to sacrifice my health when I feel behind at work.

But then I call my parents and hear their appreciation for making time to talk with them.

It reminds me of why it's worth it.

And, most importantly, seeing employees put their family before work.

Because as the **CEO**, I set the example.

Vague pain statement:

It's rough.

I take these tough actions:

Every morning I hit the gym at 4:30 am.
Then get to the office by 7 a.m. to write for two hours.

To help those I care about:

I do it because it makes me a better employer.

Balance is hard to find:

As a young entrepreneur running a company, it's hard to find balance.

Between these two important things:

You want to be at the top of your game for your employees, but you don't want to sacrifice your health.

Have to champion everything:

You have to do it all.

You want to go further:

And as a founder — you're never satisfied.

But you have limits:

You want to put more into work, but you can't.
There will always be more tasks.

Make sure to get the rights things done:

I ensure to come home with an hour to talk to family and friends.

It doesn't always work out that way:

But this doesn't always happen.

As in this tangible example:

Back when we only had four people on the team, we once signed several clients in a day for BAMF Media.

I suffered with these tangible examples:

For a week, I didn't get any sleep and missed every workout.

I almost didn't make it back:

It took me an entire month to get back into my routine.
I vowed I would never do this again.

Now I'm better at what I do:

Today, I set better expectations for my clients.
Rather than say "today," I'll say "two weeks."

I still feel the pressure:

I'd be lying if I stated that I no longer get pressured to sacrifice my health when I feel behind at work.

I don't make the mistake because I do [X]:

But then I call my parents and hear their appreciation for making time to talk with them.
It reminds me of why it's worth it.

And, of course, this reason, too:

And, most importantly, seeing employees put their family before work.

Tied into this inspirational line about my responsibility:

Because as the CEO, I set the example.

FOUGHT TRADITION TO ACHIEVE SUCCESS

— Ben Lee

I dropped out of college.

"If I see you texting again, I'll kick you out of class."

The teacher scolded me in front of everyone.

I answered, "I'm busy calculating shipping costs to send fine art to Dubai."

He replied, "What does that even mean?"

I was hustling on eBay.

At first, we weren't making any money.

Then sales starting coming once we found our niche — collector items and pop art.

After I sold a Mr. Brainwash original for $12,000 to a collector in Dubai, it hit me.

I didn't need college.

So I left.

I struggled with dropping out for over a year and a half.

What would my future employers think?

What would my parents think?

But that one sale was all the validation I needed.

I remember my Dad saying, "Ben, you need to go to law school. That's where you'll be successful."

The truth is school would never give me the ROI in business that the real world would.

It would only give me debt.

So I wrote a check for my last semester at Loyola Marymount University paying it off in full.

A month later, I founded the most successful online learning resource for law students.

If you're not satisfied with where you are, then reach higher.

I could've wasted the next couple of years in college.

Instead, I became an entrepreneur.

I made a huge life decision against the traditional path:

I dropped out of college.

Here's the exact moment I knew it would happen:

"If I see you texting again, I'll kick you out of class."
The teacher scolded me in front of everyone.
I answered, "I'm busy calculating shipping costs to send fine art to Dubai."
He replied, "What does that even mean?"

— I was working outside of tradition: —————

I was hustling on eBay. At first, we weren't making any money.

— I had a lot of success with these two tangible ———
examples:

*Then sales starting coming once we found our niche - collector items
and pop art.*
*After I sold a Mr. Brainwash original for $12,000 to a collector in Dubai,
it hit me.*

— I didn't need tradition: ————————

I didn't need college. So I left.

— It took me this exact amount of time to make the ———
decision:

I struggled with dropping out for over a year and a half.

I had these self-conscious thoughts about it:

What would my future employers think? What would my parents think?

That small success propelled me forward:

But that one sale was all the validation I needed.

I even had close friends/family say stuff like this to keep me in tradition:

I remember my Dad saying, "Ben, you need to go to law school. That's where you'll be successful."

It wasn't true because of this:

The truth is school would never give me the ROI in business that the real world would.

I'd only get negative results:

It would only give me debt.

I left in a memorable way:

So I wrote a check for my last semester at Loyola Marymount University paying it off in full.

Then I became successful:

A month later, I founded the most successful online learning resource for law students.

Realization:

If you're not satisfied with where you are, then reach higher.

Backed by a tangible example of the opportunity cost I faced:

I could've wasted the next couple of years in college. Instead, I became an entrepreneur.

FOUND OPPORTUNITY IN THE DUST THEY LEFT ME IN

— BEN LEE

My employer outsourced my job.

I was a young, hungry technical sales guy.

I was 20 and making six figures working with a world-class team.

My boss had said, "Ben, you're the most badass employee without a CS degree."

Then out of the blue, I wasn't getting included in dev calls.

I could feel the ground slipping beneath me.

Then it happened.

The entire team received a ticket to an upcoming conference except me.

"Ben, we should talk."

At that moment, I took the reins.

"You didn't give me proper notice — fly me out."

And they did.

Then fired me.

I used that trip to found a company, Neon Roots.

Today our partners include Salesforce, Spotify, and Snoop Dogg.

I remember my first prospect saying, "How can you recruit the best engineers when you aren't coding?"

"Recruiting isn't about engineering — it's about people."

They passed.

That year, I hit over a million dollars in revenue because I inspired the world's best engineers to work for me.

This is why companies struggle to stay relevant - they forget everything is about people.

If you don't fit their mold, they kick you to the curb.

Culture comes first.

At Rootstrap, we do things differently.

Thank you, Fernando Colman, for allowing me to create a culture that made us one of the top employers in America.

My team member did this negative thing to me:

My employer outsourced my job.

— At the time, I was hustling to make it:

I was a young, hungry technical sales guy.

— I was doing well relative to my circumstances:

I was 20 and making six figures working with a world-class team.

— Even people I respected said so:

My boss had said, "Ben, you're the most badass employee without a CS degree."

— Then they cut off the opportunities:

Then out of the blue, I wasn't getting included in dev calls.

— I could see it happening:

I could feel the ground slipping beneath me.
Then it happened.

— I was left in the dust: —

The entire team received a ticket to an upcoming conference except me.

— I found opportunity in the dust: —

"Ben, we should talk." At that moment, I took the reins. "You didn't give me proper notice - fly me out." And they did. Then fired me.

— I used it to propel my success: —

I used that trip to found a company, Neon Roots.

— Now we're successful with these tangible credibility — points:

Today our partners include Salesforce, Spotify, and Snoop Dogg.

— I remember people still doubting me: —

I remember my first prospect saying, "How can you recruit the best engineers when you aren't coding?"
"Recruiting isn't about engineering - it's about people."

— I've lost opportunities: ——————————————————————

They passed.

— But it didn't matter because I came out on top: ——————

That year, I hit over a million dollars in revenue because I inspired the world's best engineers to work for me.

— You won't do well if you don't value hustle and ——————
   uniqueness:

This is why companies struggle to stay relevant - they forget everything is about people.
If you don't fit their mold, they kick you to the curb.
Culture comes first.

— Today, my team does it the opposite way: ——————————

At Rootstrap, we do things differently.

Thank you to a particular current team member for contributing to a 3rd party credibility that shows we're not like the people who left me in the dust:

Thank you, Fernando Colman, for allowing me to create a culture that made us one of the top employers in America.

I quit my job.

I ran out of savings.

I bootstrapped down and moved into my Dad's tiny apartment.

Without much space, we slept in the same room.

During this time, I learning something beautiful:

Success and happiness parallel how much value we create for others.

Not how many books we read, podcasts we listen to, or YouTube videos we watch.

The problem. I had no skills. I had no money.

With few options, I began writing for many hours every day.

To focus, I stopped…
> › Talking to friends who didn't help me create value
> › Opening my Facebook News Feed
> › Paying attention to politics
> › Watching T.V. and Netflix
> › Going out to eat

First, I wrote on my blog.

As I became a better writer, I contributed to publications.

People began to recognize and respect my ability to create value.

I left my low-pay copywriting job to work for a Facebook software company and moved out of my Dad's apartment.

I then took a job as the VP of marketing for an events company spread across five cities, then eventually, I became the head of growth for a VC firm.

Now, I'm a founder of two companies and a 15,000-person community.

If your life is not on a successful track, then ask yourself:

Am I a consumer or a creator?

Start the piece by drilling down into the problem and "knife twisting" in a total of eight words:

I quit my job. I ran out of savings.

Explain the negative outcomes and release vulnerability within the next three lines:

I bootstrapped down and moved into my Dad's tiny apartment. Without much space, we slept in the same room."

Dive into the aha moment:

During this time, I learning something beautiful:
Success and happiness parallel how much value we create for others.

Reiterate a clearer picture of the problem with more confidence:

Not how many books we read, podcasts we listen to, or YouTube videos
we watch.
The problem. I had no skills. I had no money.

Dive into the sacrifices you needed to make to solve the problem:

With few options, I began writing for many hours every day.
To focus, I stopped…

> *Talking to friends who didn't help me create value*
> *Opening my Facebook News Feed*
> *Paying attention to politics*
> *Watching T.V. and Netflix*
> *Going out to eat*

The result of the sacrifices (first step of the hero's journey):

First, I wrote on my blog.

Escalate the first step to the second step fast:

As I became a better writer, I contributed to publications.

Beneficial outcome:

People began to recognize and respect my ability to create value.

Problem solved:

I left my low-pay copywriting job to work for a Facebook software company and moved out of my Dad's apartment.

Escalate the benefit to give more credibility to the learning:

I then took a job as the VP of marketing for an events company spread across five cities, then eventually, I became the head of growth for a VC firm.

Say directly or imply how you give back from your learning:

Now, I'm a founder of two companies and a 15,000-person community.

Ask yourself this question if you have similar problems:

If your life is not on a successful track, then ask yourself:
Am I a consumer or a creator?

Hey LinkedIn friends,

Are there any funded founders working in tech?

I created a private but free Facebook community for tech startup founders that have raised money.

We're sharing proven fundraising, marketing and operational strategies like:
> How to optimize your investor deck
> How to nurture potential investors
> How to hire early employees
> How to optimize your acquisition channels
> How to practice a healthy work/startup life balance

Some brilliant-minded investors in my network from Draper Associates, AngelList, Graph Ventures, and 500 Startups are already in the group along with other founders in tech.

Interested in joining?

Comment "interested" and I'll send you an invitation link via private message.

Personalized intro for the platform:

Hey LinkedIn friends,

Relevant question to your network:

Are there any funded founders working in tech?

A community benefit you provide:

I created a private but free Facebook community for tech startup founders that have raised money.

The value in the community:

We're sharing proven fundraising, marketing and operational strategies like:

› *How to optimize your investor deck*
› *How to nurture potential investors*
› *How to hire early employees*
› *How to optimize your acquisition channels*
› *How to practice a healthy work/startup life balance*

Add credibility with brand names:

Some brilliant-minded investors in my network from Draper Associates, AngelList, Graph Ventures, and 500 Startups are already in the group along with other founders in tech.

The ask:

Interested in joining?

Details on how to participate:

Comment "interested" and I'll send you an invitation link via private message.

Hey LinkedIn friends,

I need your help with choosing a book cover.

I've already written the book (300+ pages)

It's the most comprehensive book ever written on growth hacking case studies from the best marketers and founders.

And this is the last piece.

Comment with which cover you like the most.

Personalized intro:

Hey LinkedIn friends,

Ask for what you need help with:

I need your help with choosing a book cover.

Explain you already made a huge investment:

I've already written the book (300+ pages)

Why it's valuable:

It's the most comprehensive book ever written on growth hacking case studies from the best marketers and founders.

Why their contribution is important (play to scarcity):

And this is the last piece.

Help me decide with this low barrier to entry for feedback:

Comment with which cover you like the most.

SENDING OUT PROPOSALS

Wish you had a network of 6000+ founders and C-level executives?

I recently did another soft launch of my membership community. Mostly word-of-mouth right now.

I'm taking people step by step of how I reversed engineered all of this in the last twelve months:
1. Facebook to build one of the most active communities of founders (15000+ members)
2. Quora to become a top writer with over 10 million views
3. The consistency to output over 1,200 pieces of content
4. LinkedIn to get over 25 million views on my content
5. Launching two 6-figure companies in one month

The program is 100% refundable within the first 30 days.

If you want to know how I'll do all of this for you, then comment below "interested" and I'll send you the details.

Ask a broad question most of your target market would say yes to:
Wish you had a network of 6000+ founders and C-level executives?

Tell them you released something secret:

I recently did another soft launch of my membership community. Mostly word-of-mouth right now.

That it will help them get these tangible KPIs:

I'm taking people step by step of how I reversed engineered all of this in the last twelve months:
1. Facebook to build one of the most active communities of founders (15000+ members)
2. Quora to become a top writer with over 10 million views
3. The consistency to output over 1,200 pieces of content
4. LinkedIn to get over 25 million views on my content
5. Launching two 6-figure companies in one month

I'm not selling. It's risk free:

The program is 100% refundable within the first 30 days.

Now ask them to show interest with a low barrier of entry:

If you want to know how I'll do all of this for you, then comment below "interested" and I'll send you the details.

SELL BEFORE YOU BUILD

After launching our agency a month ago, we recently landed a big enough client to hire a couple of more employees.

We were pitching this client before we even had an LLC, office, or logo.

We're always selling because we know that's what it takes to have the opportunity to create results.

Rather than waiting as most founders do, we instill selling as a natural part of our culture. We think a sales mentality helps people understand that opportunities are everywhere.

You don't need the product or even a company.

You can sell to create anything you want.

That's why crowdfunding exists.

As long you deliver on your promise, both parties will be happy.

Start with a positive announcement:

After launching our agency a month ago, we recently landed a big enough client to hire a couple of more employees.

Talk about how you hustled to make it happen in a counterintuitive way:

We were pitching this client before we even had an LLC, office, or logo.

Why we did it this way — it works:

We're always selling because we know that's what it takes to have the opportunity to create results.

We think differently — it's part of our culture:

Rather than waiting as most founders do, we instill selling as a natural part of our culture. We think a sales mentality helps people understand that opportunities are everywhere.

It starts with knowing that these core principles are true:

You don't need the product or even a company.
You can sell to create anything you want.

If they weren't, then this thing you know that is true wouldn't exist:

That's why crowdfunding exists.

There's an exception, but don't be that exception:

As long you deliver on your promise, both parties will be happy.

MY SACRIFICES ARE NOT SACRIFICES

As a twenty-six-year-old founder, I remember all the

Netflix shows I tuned out.

Bar invites I dismissed.

Festivals I skipped.

And late Saturday nights walking out of a coworking space and seeing a line outside of a popular club across the street.

What I'm missing out on is nothing compared to the thousands of entrepreneurs in my community who want to change the world.

And if I lend my hand, I can give them and the millions they reach thousands of memories.

I don't make sacrifices.

I help people.

As someone who's at the beginning of their journey:

As a twenty-six-year-old founder, I remember all the

All these experiences I didn't take part in:

Netflix shows I tuned out.
Bar invites I dismissed.
Festivals I skipped.

Particularly this tangible example:

And late Saturday nights walking out of a coworking space and seeing a line outside of a popular club across the street.

It's nothing compared to the work I'm doing:

What I'm missing out on is nothing compared to the thousands of entrepreneurs in my community who want to change the world.

Because I can give people everything I missed:

And if I lend my hand, I can give them and the millions they reach thousands of memories.

It's not a painful choice; it's more rewarding:

I don't make sacrifices.
I help people.

HOW TO SPOT INTELLIGENT PEOPLE

How to spot intelligent people:

They ask you questions.

When you answer, they ask you more.

When you start using big words, they ask for clarification.

When they can't understand anything you're saying, they ask for you to explain it to them as if they were a five-year-old.

When you say something intriguing, they write it down in their notebook or phone.

These people are not naturally more intelligent. They're better learners which makes them more intelligent.

Why do they learn better?

They're genuinely curious and ask questions from a humble standpoint. I've met billionaires who've said, "explain it to me as if I were a five-year-old."

This simple phrase has changed my life when it comes to learning.

As soon as you stop asking questions, you stop learning.

As soon as you stop writing down ideas, you forget them.

The hardest part of becoming intelligent is not bullshitting yourself about what you know; it's being humble enough to ask questions. If you can do this, then people will see you as intelligent, too.

A know-it-all statement (ex. how to identify wealthy people):

How to spot intelligent people:

The act in a few short words:

They ask you questions.

They persist:

When you answer, they ask you more.

They keep persisting:

When you start using big words, they ask for clarification.

To the point where they sacrifice all ego:

When they can't understand anything you're saying, they ask for you to explain it to them as if they were a five-year-old.

They savor the benefit:

When you say something intriguing, they write it down in their notebook or phone.

It's not nature; it's nurture:

These people are not naturally more intelligent. They're better learners which makes them more intelligent.

Why is this the case?

Why do they learn better?

Because they sacrifice all ego and here's a tangible example from a credible source:

They're genuinely curious and ask questions from a humble standpoint. I've met billionaires who've said, "explain it to me as if I were a five-year-old."

This has changed my life:

This simple phrase has changed my life when it comes to learning.

— Break it down into two key actions with their result: —

As soon as you stop asking questions, you stop learning.
As soon as you stop writing down ideas, you forget them.

— You need to take a strong stance to get the results: —

The hardest part of becoming intelligent is not bullshitting yourself about what you know; it's being humble enough to ask questions. If you can do this, then people will see you as intelligent, too.

How to identify a liar:

Ask them about a failure.

I took a call with the founder of a marketing agency who wanted to partner with our venture capital firm.

The founder wouldn't stop talking about the company's accomplishments.

"We've made our clients a lot of money. We work with the best startups."

He wasn't explaining how he could help us.

He kept talking about himself.

I was fishy about his approach, so I used my trick to identify liars.

"Tell me about a time when your client didn't get their desired result. A time when you failed."

I was looking to see if he would take responsibility for the failure. If he did, then I'd consider his proposal.

After each of his statements, here's what I thought:

"They were the worst company."

He should've said, "We didn't vet the company."

"They had unrealistic expectations."

He should've said, "We didn't set the right expectations."

"They didn't have enough leverage with their assets."

He should've said, "We didn't correctly assess the value of their assets."

I stopped listening.

Knowing how to deal with failure is a critical piece of success. If you blame others, then you won't improve.

It shows you have an ego and fail to take responsibility when things go south.

That's a sign you're a liar.

— A know-it-all statement (how to identify wealthy people):

How to identify a liar:

— The act in a few short words: —

Ask them about a failure.

— Here's a tangible example with high stakes: —

I took a call with the founder of a marketing agency who wanted to partner with our venture capital firm.

The problem happened with this person:

The founder wouldn't stop talking about the company's accomplishments.

A tangible, conversational example of the problem:

"We've made our clients a lot of money. We work with the best startups."

They should've done this:

He wasn't explaining how he could help us.

Instead they did this:

He kept talking about himself.

To make the right judgment, I used this tactic:

I was fishy about his approach, so I used my trick to identify liars.

I ask about a specific time that would reveal their perception of responsibility:

"Tell me about a time when your client didn't get their desired result. A time when you failed."
I was looking to see if he would take responsibility for the failure. If he did, then I'd consider his proposal.

They gave me the wrong statements. Here's what they should've said:

After each of his statements, here's what I thought: "They were the worst company." He should've said, "We didn't vet the company." "They had unrealistic expectations." He should've said, "We didn't set the right expectations." "They didn't have enough leverage with their assets." He should've said, "We didn't correctly assess the value of their assets."

It was over before it ended. I made my decision:

I stopped listening.

Don't do that if you want success:

Knowing how to deal with failure is a critical piece of success. If you blame others, then you won't improve.

Because it reveals this negative quality:

It shows you have an ego and fail to take responsibility when things go south.

That means the negative characteristic in #1:

That's a sign you're a liar.

HOW TO IDENTIFY CREATIVE PEOPLE

How to identify creative people.

They repeat what you say with examples.

They use analogies, synonyms, and metaphors.

When conversations become complex —

They make them simple.

Because creatives don't tell people facts or opinions.

They show them.

By using examples to provide empathy.

Few can remember the definition of $e = mc^2$.

Because even though Albert Einstein was one of the best physicists — he was even better at turning observations into numbers.

His inspiration didn't come from equations.

It came from real life examples.

And imagination.

These people are not naturally more creative.

They're more empathetic which makes them more creative.

The hardest part?

Being vulnerable enough to show how you feel with examples.

And curious enough to explore them.

Because people don't remember what you say.

They remember how they felt.

A know-it-all statement (how to identify wealthy people):

How to identify creative people.

The act in a few short words:

They repeat what you say with examples.

With these tangible examples:

They use analogies, synonyms, and metaphors.

When a problem arises:

When conversations become complex —

They solve it:

They make them simple.

For these reasons:

Because creatives don't tell people facts or opinions. They show them.
By using examples to provide empathy.

Here's a tangible example with celebrity credibility:

Few can remember the definition of e = mc². Because even though Albert
Einstein was one of the best physicists — he was even better at turning
observations into numbers. His inspiration didn't come from equations.
It came from real life examples. And imagination.

They have a quality that's not what you'd think:

These people are not naturally more creative.
They're more empathetic which makes them more creative.

The quality you need isn't easy to express:

The hardest part? Being vulnerable enough to show how you feel with examples. And curious enough to explore them.

The reason it's important:

Because people don't remember what you say.
They remember how they felt.

APPRECIATION OF A MEETING

Today, I had a meeting in LinkedIn's lobby in San Francisco.

I needed help.

The last few months, I've been struggling to get my community members to write copy like I do.

I sought help from the best — Neville Medhora.

He owns the most famous copywriting course online and was the mastermind behind AppSumo's emails.

I explained my issue:

"Not everyone in my community is catching up to speed with writing copy like I do."

His answer:

"Don't expect them to become like you. Expect them to become great in their own ways - ways you may not even be a professional in."

For the longest time, I wanted my mentees to become like me.

What I learned: They may not write copy like I do, but that doesn't mean it's bad copy.

It's often a beautiful sign — they've found their voice, not mine.

Use credibility to set a time and place of your meeting:

Today, I had a meeting in LinkedIn's lobby in San Francisco.

Express the pain in a few words:

I needed help.

Dig the knife in:

The last few months, I've been struggling to get my community members to write copy like I do.

Tie this into the "why" behind your meeting:

I sought help from the best - Neville Medhora.

Expand on the person's credibility:

He owns the most famous copywriting course online and was the mastermind behind AppSumo's emails.

Dive back into your problem with a tangible conversation piece:

I explained my issue:

"Not everyone in my community is catching up to speed with writing copy like I do."

The solution — using another tangible conversation piece:

His answer: "Don't expect them to become like you. Expect them to become great in their own ways - ways you may not even be a professional in."

My reflection on the problem:

For the longest time, I wanted my mentees to become like me.

I discovered this solution:

What I learned: They may not write copy like I do, but that doesn't mean it's bad copy.

The resulting aha moment:

It's often a beautiful sign — they've found their voice, not mine.

PARODY OF CHASING YOUR PASSION

My best friend left her job.

She worked for Google and had a nice, cushy salary.

Then one day, she read an article on Facebook, "10 Reasons to Chase Entrepreneurship & Travel the World"

She felt so inspired she quit her job.

She tried to become a lifestyle entrepreneur and realized it's fucken hard — way harder than anything she imagined.

Every venture of hers failed.

In only a year, she ran out of savings and moved in with her parents.

Now she writes articles like "10 Reasons to Chase Entrepreneurship & Travel the World" so other people will leave their jobs.

This way there will be a spot open for someone to hire her.

Big life change:
My best friend left her job.

Left a fantastic opportunity:
She worked for Google and had a nice, cushy salary.

Because of this cheesy inspiration many of us are exposed to every day:

Then one day, she read an article on Facebook, "10 Reasons to Chase Entrepreneurship & Travel the World"
She felt so inspired she quit her job.

They chased the "good life" then realize it's not easy:

She tried to become a lifestyle entrepreneur and realized it's fucken hard — way harder than anything she imagined.

Nothing worked out:

Every venture of hers failed.

They ended up with these tangible problems:

In only a year, she ran out of savings and moved in with her parents.

— Now they add to the cheesy reason to help other —
people make big life changes:

Now she writes articles like "10 Reasons to Chase Entrepreneurship & Travel the World" so other people will leave their jobs.

— To give them back their original opportunity: —

This way there will be a spot open for someone to hire her.

WEEKEND HUSTLE

When it's 10 p.m. in an empty co-working space, I remember why it's not luck.

I came to San Francisco a year ago with no network. And a week ago, I launched my service to help founders become social media evangelists.

We're on track for 20K MRR in our first month.

For the last year, I put every weekend, early morning, and late night into this project.

That doesn't count the four years of experience in startups and growth I had prior.

It's all worth it.

Because one day, you can separate free, build your own ship, raise your own flag, and hire your own crew.

It's the freedom to build your dream.

And I finally have a taste of it.

When I'm working harder than everyone else, I remember why I get results:

When it's 10 p.m. in an empty co-working space, I remember why it's not luck.

I started with nothing. Now I launched this service:

I came to San Francisco a year ago with no network. And a week ago, I launched my service to help founders become social media evangelists.

We're already off to an excellent start:

We're on track for 20K MRR in our first month.

I've spent all my free time dedicated to making this happen:

For the last year, I put every weekend, early morning, and late night into this project.

This doesn't cover the last [period of time] of relevant experience:

That doesn't count the four years of experience in startups and growth I had prior.

I wouldn't have done it differently:

It's all worth it.

Because one day you can do your own thing with this great metaphor:

Because one day, you can separate free, build your own ship, raise your own flag, and hire your own crew.

The realization of the goal:

It's the freedom to build your dream.

I'm almost there:

And I finally have a taste of it.

PROMOTING AN EVENT

I went $25,000 into the hole.

A year and a half ago, I brought ten people together in a conference room to talk about growth marketing.

As I did this week after week because I love helping startups, we grew fast.

We went from hosting events in a small office space to a coworking space, and eventually, the Nasdaq.

To complement our in-person community, I made an online community — now it's one of the most renowned communities for startups.

I continued to spend my money on building the Badass Marketers & Founders' brand because I knew one thing:

When I found the right ask, the community would support me.

And it did.

I used my community to start two companies: a digital agency, and a membership program.

Then I leveraged it for a presentation in front of 30,000 registrants of the largest growth marketing event ever — hosted by Growth Tribe. It's happening this week!

I get to present right next to the best growth marketers and hackers, including Savvas Zortikis, co-founder of Viral Loops.

It took a year of full-time work and losing money to see the light.

It's clear:

Your career is not about making money.

Your career is about longevity.

Chase what you can't ignore.

— I had a huge tangible problem in a few short words: —

I went $25,000 into the hole.

— I started from the bottom with this tangible scene: —

A year and a half ago, I brought ten people together in a conference room to talk about growth marketing.

— I pursued this passion every week with a positive result:

As I did this week after week because I love helping startups, we grew fast.

As we put in more effort, our community grew:

We went from hosting events in a small office space to a coworking space, and eventually, the NASDAQ.

We expanded and now we have a brand name:

To complement our in-person community, I made an online community - now it's one of the most renowned communities for startups.

I invested in the community because I believe in reciprocity:

I continued to spend my money on building the Badass Marketers & Founders' brand because I knew one thing:
When I found the right ask, the community would support me.

When I finally asked, they supported me:

And it did.

As a result, my community helped me create these cool tangible businesses:

I used my community to start two companies: a digital agency, and a membership program.

It got better. I received this tangible opportunity:

Then I leveraged it for a presentation in front of 30,000 registrants of the largest growth marketing event ever — hosted by Growth Tribe.
It's happening this week! I get to present right next to the best growth marketers and hackers, including Savvas Zortikis, co-founder of Viral Loops.

It wasn't easy. I had to persist for a long time:

It took a year of full-time work and losing money to see the light.

Here's what I learned:

It's clear:

What you want is not about X:

Your career is not about making money.

It's about Y:

Your career is about longevity.

So chase what syncs with Y:

Chase what you can't ignore.

PROMOTING AN ARTICLE

You don't need to like me.

My writing style. My use of expletives. Talking openly about my failures.

I'm unique.

I plan to stay that way.

Here's what being true to myself has done for me:

Led to my life being seen by over 25 million on LinkedIn in four months.

Inspired thousands of LinkedIn users to open their voice.

Helped others build successful businesses.

And today, it got my entire LinkedIn story featured in Forbes. I put the link to the article in the first comment:

I don't need validation from other people:

You don't need to like me.

I don't care what you think about these three semi-controversial things I do:

My writing style. My use of expletives. Talking openly about my failures.

There's only one of me:

I'm unique.

Let's keep it that way:

I plan to stay that way.

Here are the tangible benefits it's provided:

Here's what being true to myself has done for me: Led to my life being seen by over 25 million on LinkedIn in four months. Inspired thousands of LinkedIn users to open their voice. Helped others build successful businesses.

It's culminated in this one awesome thing happening in my life recently:

And today, it got my entire LinkedIn story featured in Forbes. I put the link to the article in the first comment:

DON'T SETTLE

— AARON AGIUS

In my early 30's I knew two things:
1. I didn't like the attitude that I brought home after work
2. I didn't want my kids to grow up seeing their father stressed all the time

For the next 6 months, my wife and I planned our trip to escape.

We bought tickets to Thailand with no plan on coming back.

I always thought travel hacking was a fluke, but it itched at me because if it were true — my kids deserved to see their parents happy.

In the meantime, juggling a business while planning to move felt like a jumping off a cliff while searching for the parachute.

"What would my family think?"

"Would my friends get upset because I left?"

Stop it.

There's real risk. Then there's perceived risk.
I see my friends in the rat race — they have perceived risk. Whenever they want to follow their dreams even for their kids, they can't pull it together. Instead, they pull out excuses.

I remember looking out of our villa at the beach & thinking "this is it."

We were paying pennies to live in one of the most beautiful places in the world and our kids grew up with parents who'd never been happier.

Today, we have a fully remote team with over fifty people.

The reason?

Our team deserves to take the right attitude home to their kids.

Because culture doesn't end in the workplace.

When I was this age, here are the two important realizations I had:

In my early 30's I knew two things:
1. I didn't like the attitude that I brought home after work
2. I didn't want my kids to grow up seeing their father stressed all the time

We planned a big life change to see the realizations through in a positive way:

For the next 6 months, my wife and I planned our trip to escape.

We took a drastic move:

We bought tickets to Thailand with no plan on coming back.

I was skeptical it would work, but I had to do it — for them:

I always thought travel hacking was a fluke, but it itched at me because if it were true — my kids deserved to see their parents happy.

It was scary like this metaphor:

In the meantime, juggling a business while planning to move felt like a jumping off a cliff while searching for the parachute.

I had these self-conscious thoughts:

"What would my family think?"
"Would my friends get upset because I left?"
Stop it.

Here's why you shouldn't worry:

There's real risk. Then there's perceived risk.

Don't be like these people who worry:

I see my friends in the rat race — they have perceived risk. Whenever they want to follow their dreams even for their kids, they can't pull it together. Instead, they pull out excuses.

I remember these tangible benefits from taking the risk:

I remember looking out of our villa at the beach & thinking "this is it."
We were paying pennies to live in one of the most beautiful places in the world and our kids grew up with parents who'd never been happier.

The risk led to another positive result:

Today, we have a fully remote team with over fifty people.
The reason?

It's about setting the right example for this group of people:

Our team deserves to take the right attitude home to their kids.
Because culture doesn't end in the workplace.

I GOT GREEDY
THEN LEARNED THIS VALUABLE LESSON

— Ben Lee

I lost every cent.

But I couldn't stop.

I bought my first bitcoin for $100.

I was working long hours and trading all over the world.

By 2013, I was the lead Fiverr seller teaching people how to create bitcoin wallets.

I had pioneered Cryptocurrency and came out on top.

Then it all came crashing down, hard.

Theft and fraud caused the MtGox bitcoin exchange to collapse.

I desperately tried to get it back.

I was forced to sell my Gox coins for pennies on the dollar.

I put more money down.

"If I invest more time and energy, it will turn around."

The more I gave, the more I lost.

I had nothing left.

As the CEO of three successful companies, I get hundreds of emails every day.

People want to know my Cryptocurrency investment strategy.

I never reply.

Here's the strategy for the first time:

Create a goal and a multiplier for yourself.

Stick to the plan.

When you hit your goal, get out.

As a founder, you always want to chase the next 'big thing.'

After all, that's how you got started.

But just because it's shiny, doesn't mean it will scale your business.

Founders need to understand that their employees come first.

I support over seventy full-time employees and I've never missed a payroll.

Know your limits.

Accept your losses.

And move on.

I had a problem:

I lost every cent.

— It'd only get worse:

But I couldn't stop.

— I remember when I took the risk:

I bought my first bitcoin for $100.

— It escalated fast:

I was working long hours and trading all over the world.

— Then people considered me an expert:

By 2013, I was the lead Fiverr seller teaching people how to create bitcoin wallets.

— I was at the top of my game:

I had pioneered Cryptocurrency and came out on top.

Then I lost everything:

Then it all came crashing down, hard.

Because the entire system was faulty:

Theft and fraud caused the MtGox bitcoin exchange to collapse.

I tried to cushion the damage:

I desperately tried to get it back.

But I was forced to let it all go:

I was forced to sell my Gox coins for pennies on the dollar.

Then I went in again:

I put more money down.

I had dreams it'd improve:

"If I invest more time and energy, it will turn around."

It never did:

The more I gave, the more I lost. I had nothing left.

With this credibility, I get lots of questions:

As the CEO of three successful companies, I get hundreds of emails every day.

Especially about the area where I lost everything:

People want to know my Cryptocurrency investment strategy.

I don't respond:

I never reply.

Until now:

Here's the strategy for the first time:

How to win:

Create a goal and a multiplier for yourself. Stick to the plan. When you hit your goal, get out.

It's normal to want to take risks:

As a founder, you always want to chase the next 'big thing.'

Because they sometimes work:

After all, that's how you got started.

Doesn't mean it always will:

But just because it's shiny, doesn't mean it will scale your business.

— Understand what's more important: —————

Founders need to understand that their employees come first.
I support over seventy full-time employees and I've never missed a payroll.

— Here's a simple recap of the learning lessons: ————

Know your limits. Accept your losses. And move on.

BE RESOURCEFUL
WHEN GETTING STARTED

— Ben Lee

I started my company with $1200.

That covered payroll.

We looked for office space, but couldn't afford it.

With hustle, we landed Concord Music Group as a client, the fifth largest record label with artists like Bruce Springsteen and Marilyn Mason.

They had the most expensive real estate next to Beverly Hills, 90210.

To move closer to our first major client, we found a production studio.

They were willing to barter.

They wanted web development.

We needed an office.

Not only did we save money, they referred us countless clients because we were simply "right there."

This led to working with Fox, Village Roadshow, and Steve Angello.

When we outgrew that space, we did the same thing with Snoop Dogg.

We worked out of his office for two years.

I remember clients saying, "Isn't it weird being in the same office as your client?"

I replied, "They respect our boundaries because we make it clear where they are."

This model has allowed us to stay lean and build a million-dollar agency without paying rent.

We always dreamed of having our own space.

Today, we do. It took us over three years.

Whenever you find yourself stuck.

Ask how you can change the circumstances given to you.

Because your resourcefulness will always define your steps forwards.

I didn't have much when I started:

I started my company with $1200.

Barely enough for the basics:

That covered payroll.

We couldn't afford fancy things:

We looked for office space, but couldn't afford it.

But we did land a credible source of revenue:

With hustle, we landed Concord Music Group as a client, the fifth largest record label with artists like Bruce Springsteen and Marilyn Mason.

This source of revenue had it going well for them:

They had the most expensive real estate next to Beverly Hills, 90210.

We wanted in, so we found a way to get closer:

To move closer to our first major client, we found a production studio.

We traded services:

They were willing to barter. They wanted web development. We needed an office.

It helped us get by in the early days — and even grow:

Not only did we save money, they referred us countless clients because we were simply "right there." This led to working with Fox, Village Roadshow, and Steve Angello.

We did it again:

When we outgrew that space, we did the same thing with Snoop Dogg. We worked out of his office for two years.

Others didn't understand:

I remember clients saying, "Isn't it weird being in the same office as your client?"

But we made it work:

I replied, "They respect our boundaries because we make it clear where they are."

┌─ This is the positive result: ─────────────────────────

This model has allowed us to stay lean and build a million-dollar agency without paying rent.

├─ Sure, we wanted it to be better: ─────────────────────

We always dreamed of having our own space.

├─ Today, it is — now that we paid our dues: ────────────

Today, we do. It took us over three years.

├─ If you find yourself in similar shoes, then ask yourself ─
[X]:

Whenever you find yourself stuck.
Ask how you can change the circumstances given to you.

├─ For this simple reason: ──────────────────────────────

Because your resourcefulness will always define your steps forwards.

RESPECT YOUR COMPETITORS

— Ben Lee

I first met my lawyer when he tried to sue me.

I was running a service consultancy for startups.

Working with my first client, my developer left the project and went on a cruise.

The next day, I woke up with an invoice for $17,000.

I disputed it.

The code was awful.

He missed every deadline.

And I had to hire a replacement.

He replied, "I coded the work and whether you choose to use it is your problem, not mine."

I let my ego get the best of me and threatened to sue.

In return, he hired the best lawyer in San Francisco for labor disputes.

When I read the letter from his lawyer, I knew I had lost.

The guy was a pro.

And I couldn't afford to fight him.

They asked to be paid in full by Monday or they'd take me to court.

I paid and almost went bankrupt.

Here's the twist:

Three years later, I was negotiating a major contract with Salesforce for Neon Roots.

It took six months to get in the same room as them. I needed legal counsel to review the contracts.

I told my co-founder, "I know where to find the best lawyer."

I called the lawyer who tried to sue me.

He negotiated the contract and got us an incredible deal in two days.

Six years later, Gabriel Levine is still my lawyer.

That $17,000 was the best investment I ever made.
If you can't beat them, hire them.

Ironic statement of how you met someone:

I first met my lawyer when he tried to sue me.

I was providing this service at the time:

I was running a service consultancy for startups.

And in the early stages, I experienced this bad moment with someone on my team:

Working with my first client, my developer left the project and went on a cruise.

The next day, I woke up with an invoice for $17,000.

I fought it:

I disputed it.

For these tangible reasons:

The code was awful. He missed every deadline. And I had to hire a replacement.

They didn't care with this tangible conversational statement:

He replied, "I coded the work and whether you choose to use it is your problem, not mine."

I pursued the case further:

I let my ego get the best of me and threatened to sue.

They partnered with the best against me:

In return, he hired the best lawyer in San Francisco for labor disputes.

I lost the fight. I had no chance:

When I read the letter from his lawyer, I knew I had lost. The guy was a pro. And I couldn't afford to fight him. They asked to be paid in full by Monday or they'd take me to court.

I almost lost everything:

I paid and almost went bankrupt.
Here's the twist:

After time had passed, I was in the middle of a huge opportunity:

Three years later, I was negotiating a major contract with Salesforce for Neon Roots. It took six months to get in the same room as them. I needed legal counsel to review the contracts.

I needed help and knew where to find it:

I told my co-founder, "I know where to find the best lawyer."

I called the person who helped my bad team member:

I called the lawyer who tried to sue me.

They did a fantastic job with this tangible example:

He negotiated the contract and got us an incredible deal in two days.

Today, I still work with them:

Six years later, Gabriel Levine is still my lawyer.

That's the best mistake I've ever made:

That $17,000 was the best investment I ever made.

The learning lesson:

If you can't beat them, hire them.

GIVE ADVICE FROM EXPERIENCE

I'm a 26-year-old founder.

And I won't listen to your advice.

Every day I get hundreds of comments telling me how to build my company.

Most don't come from experience.

They've never worked or founded an early-stage startup.

These startups are not rainbows and sunshine.

It takes sweat, tears, and overtime.

And countless failures.

I don't expect most people to know what it's like.

To move cities to live with your co-founder.

Build a company on a credit card.

Have every friend call you crazy.

Then still create an agency, BAMF Media, on track to employ over thirty people in its first year — entirely bootstrapped.

The hard truth: Giving advice is free.

Giving advice from experience is earned.

Block out 99% of noise to focus on what matters.

And that's listening to people who've been in your shoes.

Then made it out alive.

State who you are with age:
I'm a 26-year-old founder.

Be controversial to your age:
And I won't listen to your advice.

All these people want me to listen to them:
Every day I get hundreds of comments telling me how to build my company.

Here's the problem:
Most don't come from experience.

For this tangible reason:

They've never worked or founded an early-stage startup.

The cold truth with a metaphor:

These startups are not rainbows and sunshine.

Tangible examples:

It takes sweat, tears, and overtime.

Dig into the pain:

And countless failures.

It's a lonely journey:

I don't expect most people to know what it's like.

── I had to take this risk: ──────────────

To move cities to live with your co-founder.

── Then this risk: ──────────────────

Build a company on a credit card.

── Then this negative thing happened: ────────

Have every friend call you crazy.

── It didn't matter because we made it a reality in the best ──
way:

*Then still create an agency, BAMF Media, on track to employ over thirty
people in its first year — entirely bootstrapped.*

── What nobody wants to hear, but is universally true: ──────

The hard truth: Giving advice is free. Giving advice from experience is earned.

If you want to change your life, then take this specific
action:

Block out 99% of noise to focus on what matters.

Expand on the action with a metaphor:

*And that's listening to people who've been in your shoes. Then made it out
alive.*

FIRST EMPLOYEE TAKING A RISK ON YOU

I paid my first employee almost nothing.

He lost his apartment.

And yet, he decided to work with us.

I wanted to pay him more.

Especially because he had years of marketing experience.

The problem: we only had one client.

And I didn't even have enough money to take a salary for myself.

But I did have enough for rent and an individual who believed in us.

We were desperate for talent.

And had more than enough leads to fill our pipeline.

When he interviewed with us, I said, "We can't pay you what you want."

He replied, "I understand."

"You have to take a bet on our momentum."

And he did.

Hendry saw what we saw.

A co-founding team with veteran experience.

Not enough helping hands.

And most importantly, a company that had yet to fit inside its brand.

We run a community of over 15,000 marketers and founders.

And reach two million people every week with content.

So we decided to bootstrap BAMF Media.

In the next three months, our first employee took the wheel.

He created a task management system.

Then automated our sales system.

And even jumped on calls to land clients.

In that time, we grew from three to twelve employees.

And he was promoted three times.

When it comes to startups, what you get paid is secondary.

It's about the people.

The culture.

Momentum.

--- Something you should not do to a subordinate: ---

I paid my first employee almost nothing.

Make it even worse:

He lost his apartment.

The person didn't care:

And yet, he decided to work with us.

I wanted to lend a hand especially because they deserved it:

I wanted to pay him more. Especially because he had years of marketing experience.

Here's why I couldn't:

The problem: we only had one client.

I was suffering too with these tangible examples:

And I didn't even have enough money to take a salary for myself.
But I did have enough for rent and an individual who believed in us.

It had to happen:

We were desperate for talent.
And had more than enough leads to fill our pipeline.

I let him know upfront with this tangible conversation piece:

When he interviewed with us, I said, "We can't pay you what you want."
He replied, "I understand."

I told them that they need to take a risk on us:

"You have to take a bet on our momentum." And he did.

They did it because our visions aligned with these tangible examples:

Hendry saw what we saw. A co-founding team with veteran experience.
Not enough helping hands. And most importantly, a company that had yet
to fit inside its brand. We run a community of over 15,000 marketers and
founders. And reach two million people every week with content.

— Because of those examples, we knew we'd become —
successful:

So we decided to bootstrap BAMF Media.

— The risk paid off with these tangible examples: —

In the next three months, our first employee took the wheel. He created a task management system. Then automated our sales system. And even jumped on calls to land clients.

— As a result, the team had this benefit: —

In that time, we grew from three to twelve employees.

— And they got a benefit that made up for all their risk: —

And he was promoted three times.

— Here's my controversial realization: —

When it comes to startups, what you get paid is secondary.
It's about the people. The culture. Momentum.

I took another offer.

Because you don't pay enough.

I hear this all the time when hiring.

We're a startup.

We pay people competitive salaries for specialists.

The problem: You hire people who were once managers.

Because they don't have anyone to manage in a five or ten-person startup — they'll take a pay cut.

It's a short-term sacrifice.

To be a part of a better culture, and the core group of people who'll make a shared vision a reality.

In the early stages, if a candidate dismisses us because they're looking for a corporate or managerial salary, then we win.

They would've never fit in anyways.

It saves us the pain of letting them go later.

The truth: if you deserve managerial pay, then a startup is the place to prove it by scaling yourself.

When you apply to work for an early-stage startup — you start fresh.

You're choosing a new culture.

To define it.

To lead it

—— I did something controversial: ———————
I took another offer.

—— Because of this controversial reason outside of my ——
control:
Because you don't pay enough. I hear this all the time when hiring.

—— The reality is we don't have a choice: ——————
We're a startup.

—— But to create this controversy for these reasons: ——
We pay people competitive salaries for specialists.
The problem: You hire people who were once managers.
Because they don't have anyone to manage in a five or ten-person startup -
they'll take a pay cut.

The good news:

It's a short-term sacrifice. To be a part of a better culture, and the core group of people who'll make a shared vision a reality.

So if the controversy does happen, we'll have a good result for this simple reason:

In the early stages, if a candidate dismisses us because they're looking for a corporate or managerial salary, then we win.

Explain the reason:

They would've never fit in anyways.
It saves us the pain of letting them go later.

The reality of the situation is that it's up to the "victim" to prove themselves:

The truth: if you deserve managerial pay, then a startup is the place to prove it by scaling yourself.

They know what they're getting into:

When you apply to work for an early-stage startup - you start fresh.

For these benefits:

You're choosing a new culture. To define it. To lead it.

QUESTION THE MAJORITY

Everyone stood up.

I sat down.

I was boarding a plane to Chicago.

And each person had an assigned seat.

It didn't matter where you were in line.

Your seat would be there for you.

Still, people chose to stand in line and complain about waiting.

Rather than join, I worked on my laptop.

And boarded last.

I took my assigned seat with zero wait time.

And I got an entire hour of work done.

This happens every time I fly.

When everyone moves in one direction, we're often quick to follow.

No matter how little sense it makes.

When you see a line, don't look for your place.

Pause, reflect, and ask why you should stand in it.

What the majority did:

Everyone stood up.

I did the opposite:

I sat down.

Here's when and where it happened:

I was boarding a plane to Chicago.
And each person had an assigned seat.

Here's the irony:

It didn't matter where you were in line.
Your seat would be there for you.

They chose the wrong decision:

Still, people chose to stand in line and complain about waiting.

Instead of following, I did this:

Rather than join, I worked on my laptop. And boarded last.

And got this benefit:

I took my assigned seat with zero wait time. And I got an entire hour of work done. This happens all the time: This happens every time I fly.

It proves this fallacy about humans:

When everyone moves in one direction, we're often quick to follow. No matter how little sense it makes.

Next time do what I did:

When you see a line, don't look for your place. Pause, reflect, and ask why you should stand in it.

STAY NIMBLE FOR OPPORTUNITIES

I slept on a couch.

Then upgraded to a mattress.

This was ten years of my life.

I love my parents. They would do anything and everything for me.

But we didn't have a lot of money.

At dinner with one of our largest clients, they asked, "What did your bedroom look like as a kid?"

My mind went blank.

My co-founder went on explaining his childhood room.

He had posters of all his heroes.

And surf boards.

Everything a kid would want.

I never had a bedroom or even a bed until years after college.

This is why I've survived in startup life for so long.

I've moved over ten times.

And had ten startup jobs.

When I got fired.

I could pack up and move to another city in the same day.

When I quit.

I could do the same.

When I met my future co-founder, Houston Golden, it took me one day to pack up everything in San Francisco to work with him in Los Angeles.

We're often in a hurry to add things to our lives to feel validated.

Then when the right opportunity appears, we're stuck.

I stayed light on my feet.

And looked inwards.

I found my validation in work, and relationships.

When you're early in your career, realize there are thousands of opportunities.

You'll only see the them if you can move fast to find what you love.

┌─ **I didn't have much:** ──────────────────────────
│ *I slept on a couch.*
│
│
│
│
│
│
└──

I got a small improvement:

Then upgraded to a mattress.

This happened over a length of time:

This was ten years of my life.

It wasn't these people's' faults for this reason:

I love my parents. They would do anything and everything for me.

Here's the vulnerable problem we had:

But we didn't have a lot of money.

The problem got unknowingly brought up in conversation:

At dinner with one of our largest clients, they asked, "What did your bedroom look like as a kid?" My mind went blank.

— I heard someone say they had the opposite with these —
tangible examples:

My co-founder went on explaining his childhood room. He had posters of all his heroes. And surf boards.

— It was the best it could be: —————————————

Everything a kid would want.

— Not my life with these tangible examples: —————

I never had a bedroom or even a bed until years after college.

— It's led to this positive outcome: ——————

This is why I've survived in startup life for so long.

— Even through all of these obstacles: ——————

I've moved over ten times. And had ten startup jobs. When I got fired.

Because of this reason:

I could pack up and move to another city in the same day.
When I quit. I could do the same.

So when an opportunity came, I took it:

When I met my future co-founder, Houston Golden, it took me one day to pack up everything in San Francisco to work with him in Los Angeles.

We get stuck because we're not willing to be vulnerable:

We're often in a hurry to add things to our lives to feel validated.
Then when the right opportunity appears, we're stuck.

By having less, I did and found what matters:

I stayed light on my feet. And looked inwards. I found my validation in work, and relationships.

The learning lesson is you need this characteristic to get this benefit:

When you're early in your career, realize there are thousands of opportunities. You'll only see the them if you can move fast to find what you love.

SOMEONE WHO HELPS YOU WHEN YOU'RE GETTING STARTED

I interviewed 150 people.

And went $25K in the hole.

This took two years of pure hustle.

Today, I'm flying to Greece to keynote a conference.

Because I paid my dues.

With only an iPhone camera, a stand, and social media.

That's all I could afford to interview people.

Two years later, I bought my first real camera.

All the while, I spent $25,000 of out-of-pocket money hosting close to one hundred events.

Brutal.

Here's the thing: I knew if I gave value every day, I'd receive more than I've ever asked for.

Because of one name: Dennis Yu

Desperate for speakers, I posted online for help.

Dennis, a well-known keynote speaker, flew across the country to give a talk at my small Meetup.

He did it for free.

And attracted a crowd three times larger than any previous talk.

I didn't even know how to thank him.

I had nothing.

That small gift of kindness gave my community momentum.

The same momentum that turned our community into over 16,000 members.

When you lend a hand, there's no telling how far it will go.

Dennis, I wish there were more people like you.

Thank you.

I did this much positive work:

I interviewed 150 people.

Had this bad outcome:

And went $25K in the hole.

It took this long:

This took two years of pure hustle.

Life is much better today:

Today, I'm flying to Greece to keynote a conference.

Because I did the work:

Because I paid my dues.

I didn't have much to do it with:

With only an iPhone camera, a stand, and social media.

Because I didn't have a lot:

That's all I could afford to interview people.

Then I upgraded:

Two years later, I bought my first real camera.

During this time, I hustled:

All the while, I spent $25,000 of out-of-pocket money hosting close to one hundred events. Brutal.

Here's why I persisted:

Here's the thing: I knew if I gave value every day, I'd receive more than I've ever asked for.

The person I owe it to:

Because of one name: Dennis Yu

I needed help:

Desperate for speakers, I posted online for help.

— They had no reason to help me, but did so anyways —
even with obstacles:

Dennis, a well-known keynote speaker, flew across the country to give a talk at my small Meetup.

— They didn't ask for anything in return: —

He did it for free.

— This led to a huge benefit: —

And attracted a crowd three times larger than any previous talk.

— There's no way to give back: —

I didn't even know how to thank him. I had nothing.

— That gift helped provide the exact solution I needed: —

That small gift of kindness gave my community momentum.

The solution that led to this tangible, positive result:

The same momentum that turned our community into over 16,000 members.

The learning lesson:

When you lend a hand, there's no telling how far it will go.

A huge thank you:

Dennis, I wish there were more people like you. Thank you.

— BEN LEE

I lost out on $100,000 last week.

We had a powerful Hollywood celebrity approach us.

The meeting took place at our office.

And he brought his business partner.

"I want to build an app."

I asked why.

"We got the next billion-dollar idea."
Red flag.

I explained that the app needed validation first.

"It's time sensitive. We need it now."

We explained that app development is a process much like building a house.

You create a blueprint and specs — then you start building.

They replied, "How long will this take?"

I said, "3 weeks for scoping."

The prospect stopped listening.

I explained, "We're not rented mules. App development takes collaboration."

"I don't want to learn about your process. I want an app."

"It looks like we won't be working together"

In one meeting, we tossed out a $100K opportunity.

It's easy to be impressed by famous people.

As your business scales, so do your clients.

But your values should never change

At the end of the day, it's your reputation on the line.

If you don't push back for what you believe in, then you'll fall for everything.

I could see my earlier self taking a deal like this one.

But today, I'm a war veteran.

And Winter is coming.

Rome didn't get built in a day.

Don't expect it to be different for a billion-dollar idea.

I lost all of this:

I lost out on $100,000 last week.

A huge person of credibility came our way:

We had a powerful Hollywood celebrity approach us.

We met them here:

The meeting took place at our office.

They weren't alone:

And he brought his business partner.

They said this:

"I want to build an app."

I asked them to explain:

I asked why.

They did:

"We got the next billion-dollar idea."

I didn't like it:

Red flag.

Here's why:

I explained that the app needed validation first.

They disagreed:

"It's time sensitive. We need it now."

So we explained our point of view:

We explained that app development is a process much like building a house. You create a blueprint and specs — then you start building.

They wanted more details:

They replied, "How long will this take?"

I gave it to them:

I said, "3 weeks for scoping."

— They stopped listening: ——————————————————

The prospect stopped listening.

— I told them there's a process: ——————————————

I explained, "We're not rented mules. App development takes collaboration."

— They didn't care: ——————————————————————

"I don't want to learn about your process. I want an app."

— So I told them it's not happening: ——————————————

"It looks like we won't be working together"

— We lost out on something huge: ——————————————

In one meeting, we tossed out a $100K opportunity.

— It's easy to say yes: ——————————————————————

It's easy to be impressed by famous people.

— For this reason: ————————————————

As your business scales, so do your clients.

— Foundations needs to remain: ————————

But your values should never change

— You got a lot to lose: ————————————

At the end of the day, it's your reputation on the line.

— Stand up because you don't want this result: ——

If you don't push back for what you believe in, then you'll fall for everything.

— A naive me would've done it: ————————

I could see my earlier self taking a deal like this one.

— I've grown: ————————————————

But today, I'm a war veteran.

The war is near:

And Winter is coming.

Here's a metaphor to better explain:

Rome didn't get built in a day.

It's no different for anyone else:

Don't expect it to be different for a billion-dollar idea.

BE RESOURCEFUL TO FIND OPPORTUNITY

— BEN LEE

We were broke.

And had one client.

The producer and DJ from Swedish House Mafia, Steve Angello.

We were on a tight deadline to release their app for the Ultra Records Winter Music Conference in Miami.

I wanted to do something nice for the team before our hyper-sprint mode.

The plan: to rent out a mansion in Uruguay.

With a small budget, I almost gave up.

As a joke, I inquired into a $20,000/week mansion on VRBO.

The next morning, I got a reply.

I visited the owner's website and saw that it was in flash.

I met her at her Santa Monica office.

"Ben, I know I need a new website, but we don't have the budget."

"Well, you're in luck. We need a house and don't have the budget."

We bartered.

And closed the deal.

Then moved into the 5-star house with a personal chef and full staff.

It motivated the employees.

And we hit our deadline for Steve Angello.

Six years later, we've done many projects with her.

And she's one of our best referral sources.

We even had my co-founder, Drew Harding, get married on her property.

You never know where you'll find business.

So ask accordingly.

We had almost nothing:

We were broke.

Only this one person with credibility:

And had one client.
The producer and DJ from Swedish House Mafia, Steve Angello.

We needed to help this person in a short time for a big reason:

We were on a tight deadline to release their app for the Ultra Records Winter Music Conference in Miami.

And I wanted to do this positive thing for us:

I wanted to do something nice for the team before our hyper-sprint mode.

Here it is:

The plan: to rent out a mansion in Uruguay.

I didn't have enough to make it happen:

With a small budget, I almost gave up.

So I took a chance:

As a joke, I inquired into a $20,000/week mansion on VRBO. The next morning, I got a reply.

Then saw opportunity with a partner:

I visited the owner's website and saw that it was in flash.
I met her at her Santa Monica office.

We had this conversation to exchange services:

"Ben, I know I need a new website, but we don't have the budget."
"Well, you're in luck. We need a house and don't have the budget."
We bartered.

It worked out:

And closed the deal. Then moved into the 5-star house with a personal chef and full staff.

With these benefits:

It motivated the employees. And we hit our deadline for Steve Angello.

The partnership continues:

Six years later, we've done many projects with her.

— With this great tangible benefit: ————————

And she's one of our best referral sources.

— We've even gone this far with it: ————————

We even had my co-founder, Drew Harding, get married on her property.

— Here's the learning lesson: ————————

You never know where you'll find business. So ask accordingly.

I SACRIFICED ALOT TO GET HERE

— BEN LEE

I run three companies and I'm 29 years old.

I had to give up a lot to get here.

I skipped countless parties and nights out with friends.

I missed out on big trips and memories.

And I can definitely say my romantic life suffered from it as well.

Few things hurt as much as watching everyone in your community build a vibrant social life while you're working late and getting up early.

But at 29, I've overseen the launch of more than 250 successful projects.

I've worked with first-time founders to help them achieve their dreams of building an app startup.

I've helped the startups I've worked with raise more than $50 million combined.

And you know what? That's just the beginning.

Because I know there's more to be done. More companies I can build. More visionaries I can help to change the world.

Yes, I may not have made the memories that my friends did.

But I traded them to make my dreams come true.

I have this huge amount of credibility:

I run three companies and I'm 29 years old.

It wasn't easy:

I had to give up a lot to get here.

I gave up all of this:

I skipped countless parties and nights out with friends.
I missed out on big trips and memories.
And I can definitely say my romantic life suffered from it as well.

I never got to have this:

Few things hurt as much as watching everyone in your community build a vibrant social life while you're working late and getting up early.

But I've had this tangible experience helping people:

But at 29, I've overseen the launch of more than 250 successful projects.
I've worked with first-time founders to help them achieve their dreams of building an app startup.
I've helped the startups I've worked with raise more than $50 million combined.

— I'm only at the start of my journey: ————————

And you know what? That's just the beginning.

— For these important reasons: ——————————

Because I know there's more to be done. More companies I can build. More visionaries I can help to change the world.

— Sure, I missed out on this: ————————————

Yes, I may not have made the memories that my friends did.

— But I got the most important thing in the end: ————

But I traded them to make my dreams come true.

— BEN LEE

I wanted to cry.

I lost my entire business.

Ratner's Deli, LLC was one of the hottest restaurants and bars in New York City.

And I was about to open one in Los Angeles.

And then, we were sued.

A group of residents known for their unfair legal settlements wanted to discuss the project.

I missed our meeting.

This led to a bloodthirsty battle.

The weapons: money, lawyers, and higher courts.

This war cost my investor hundreds of thousands of dollars.

After five years of fighting, we were on the brink of giving up.

And then, an angel came to the rescue: Victor De La Cruz.

He was tired of small business owners getting beat up by bullies in court.

And took on our case pro bono.

With his help, I got the permits and liquor license to open Ratner's Deli, LLC.

But because of the lawsuit, I no longer had the money to open.

I sold my permits.

As an entrepreneur, I know that losses are devastating.

But I also know that each one holds a lesson.

My losses gave me a better education than a Yale Law degree.

Losing the restaurant led me into to tech where I am a CEO of three companies.

One day you'll look back and realize:

The most painful moments got you to exactly where you needed to be.

Enjoy the highs.

Ride the lows.

And no matter what — keep grinding.

I was in this sad state:

I wanted to cry.

— For this horrible reason: —————————————

I lost my entire business.

— I had the best opportunity: —————————————

Ratner's Deli, LLC was one of the hottest restaurants and bars in New York City. And I was about to open one in Los Angeles.

— Then it came crumbling down because of people with —
bad intentions:

And then, we were sued. A group of residents known for their unfair legal settlements wanted to discuss the project.

— Unknowingly I made a critical mistake: —————————————

I missed our meeting.

— It led to this awful situation: —————————————

This led to a bloodthirsty battle. The weapons: money, lawyers, and higher courts.

— It cost me almost everything: ——————

This war cost my investor hundreds of thousands of dollars.

— After so much investment, we almost gave in: ——————

After five years of fighting, we were on the brink of giving up.

— I got saved by this person: ——————

And then, an angel came to the rescue: Victor De La Cruz.

— They had good character: ——————

He was tired of small business owners getting beat up by bullies in court.

— Helped us without asking anything in return: ——————

And took on our case pro bono.

— Led to this positive result: —

With his help, I got the permits and liquor license to open Ratner's Deli, LLC.

— In the end, we were left without enough to persist: —

But because of the lawsuit, I no longer had the money to open.

— I gave away everything: —

I sold my permits.

— I learned this important lesson: —

As an entrepreneur, I know that losses are devastating.
But I also know that each one holds a lesson.

— In the end, I actually won: —

My losses gave me a better education than a Yale Law degree.

── And it showed with this tangible example: ──

Losing the restaurant led me into to tech where I am a CEO of three companies.

── You'll go through it too: ──

One day you'll look back and realize:

── And come out with the same important realization: ──

The most painful moments got you to exactly where you needed to be.

── Knowing that, you should do this: ──

Enjoy the highs. Ride the lows. And no matter what — keep grinding.

FIND YOUR OBSESSION

— BEN LEE

Stop it.

Take Friday nights off.

I heard this over and again.

My entire life people called me OCD, strange, and compulsive.

When I want something to happen — it does.

I'm like The Terminator.

The problem: this attitude never fits into corporate culture. Every job I've had in larger companies people complained.

"You never come to happy hours."

"Stop working so much."

Connecting the dots looking back, my only choice was to start a company.

I talked to my co-founder the other day, and he said, "You're obsessive."

I replied, "I know."

He paused, then laughed, "No wonder you kick ass at what you do."

When hiring early-stage employees, we look for people consumed by their craft.

Coders who contribute to Stack Overflow.

Designers who dream about design.

Writers who carry notebooks.
Because finding one's obsession is life's greatest gift.
The key is to know you're obsessed. Then live it consciously.

─── Abrupt statement: ────────────────────

Stop it.

─── An often agreed upon opinion: ──────────

Take Friday nights off. I heard this over and again.

─── Negatives things people say about you: ───

My entire life people called me OCD, strange, and compulsive.

─── For this reason: ──────────────────────

When I want something to happen — it does.

Compare yourself to a powerful metaphorical person:

I'm like The Terminator.

I don't fit in — in these places:

The problem: this attitude never fits into corporate culture.

Pain point expressed with a tangible conversational piece:

Every job I've had in larger companies people complained. "You never come to happy hours." "Stop working so much."

Knowing what I know now, I realized it had to be this way:

Connecting the dots looking back, my only choice was to start a company.

This instant came up again with someone close to me:

I talked to my co-founder the other day, and he said, "You're obsessive."
I replied, "I know."

They accepted it:

He paused, then laughed, "No wonder you kick ass at what you do."

That's what we look for when adding people to our team:

When hiring early-stage employees, we look for people consumed by their craft.

Here are examples:

Coders who contribute to Stack Overflow. Designers who dream about design. Writers who carry notebooks.

It comes down to this important lesson:

Because finding one's obsession is life's greatest gift.

The catch:

The key is to know you're obsessed. Then live it consciously.

FUNNY WAY THINGS WORKED OUT IN YOUR FAVOUR

I needed a "C" to pass my college communications course.

If I didn't get a "C," I would fail to meet my college major requirements setting me back an entire semester.

Here's the problem: The semester was over, and I had a D+.

My only hope was to email the teacher asking for a bump in my grade.

I wrote an email to her explaining how my past school performance warranted a higher grade and that not passing me would only hurt an ambitious student.

When I hit send, I realized I made a *huge* mistake.

I addressed her using another teacher's name.

I tried to calm down, but then I remembered we'd spent half the semester covering email etiquette.

Shoot! What did I do?

Two days later, she emails back.

First, she addresses the glaring mistake then says she bumped my grade up to a "C" to never have me as a student again.

I went out for drinks that night.

This is by far the best mistake I've ever made.

── I needed this crucial result to get this benefit: ──

I needed a "C" to pass my college communications course.

── If I didn't, I'd be screwed: ──

If I didn't get a "C," I would fail to meet my college major requirements setting me back an entire semester.

── Here's the tangible problem: ──

Here's the problem: The semester was over, and I had a D+.

── I had one option: ──

My only hope was to email the teacher asking for a bump in my grade.

── I took it to help my case: ──

I wrote an email to her explaining how my past school performance warranted a higher grade and that not passing me would only hurt an ambitious student.

Then I screwed up — big time:

*When I hit send, I realized I made a **huge** mistake.
I addressed her using another teacher's name.*

I made a mistake that was the foundation of getting my result:

*I tried to calm down, but then I remembered we'd spent half the semester covering email etiquette. **Shoot! What did I do?***

I got a response from the person who decides my fate:

Two days later, she emails back.

They're upset, but let me move forward because they don't want to deal with me anymore:

First, she addresses the glaring mistake then says she bumped my grade up to a "C" to never have me as a student again.

I celebrated:

I went out for drinks that night.

A recap:

This is by far the best mistake I've ever made.

PERFECT DAYS

— Gilles De Clerck

I wake up at 6am.

I stretch and drink a glass of lemon water.

I read for half an hour, then get in a 20-minute workout.

I take a cold shower, drink a protein shake and brush my teeth.

On my way to work, I listen to a podcast.

In the office, I dig deep into my creative flow.

I get tons of work done and reach my goals.

On the way back home, I call my dad and do groceries.

I make myself a healthy meal, then workout.

One hour of writing and one hour of reading.

I turn the lights off and fall asleep with a big smile on my face.

I couldn't have done more. I gave my all.

I feel amazing, on top of the world.

A perfect day.

I have them sometimes, about once a week.

On other days, I wake up at 7:30.

I don't work out, my shower is hot, my podcast is music, social media fucks with my flow and I don't get my work done.

I don't read, I don't write. I order take-out and watch Netflix.

But I still sleep like a baby.

It's okay to not always have perfect days. It's okay to not always be on top of Motivation Mountain.

We tend to think of motivation as a tireless source of driving intrinsic energy and we get confused when we lose it, when we feel unmotivated.

But motivation is not a sprint, it's a marathon.

It's not giving up on trying to have perfect days.

I take hard tangible steps to improve my life in this exact order:

I wake up at 6am. I stretch and drink a glass of lemon water. I read for half an hour, then get in a 20-minute workout. I take a cold shower, drink a protein shake and brush my teeth. On my way to work, I listen to a podcast. In the office, I dig deep into my creative flow. I get tons of work done and reach my goals. On the way back home, I call my dad and do groceries. I make myself a healthy meal, then workout. One hour of writing and one hour of reading. I turn the lights off and fall asleep with a big smile on my face. I couldn't have done more. I gave my all. I feel amazing, on top of the world.

— The overall result: —————————————————

A perfect day.

— This rarely happens: —————————————————

I have them sometimes, about once a week.

— Here's what really happens with negative tangible ———
examples:

On other days, I wake up at 7:30. I don't work out, my shower is hot, my podcast is music, social media fucks with my flow and I don't get my work done. I don't read, I don't write. I order take-out and watch Netflix.

— It ends on this positive note: —————————————

But I still sleep like a baby.

— It's okay to have the negative: —————————————

It's okay to not always have perfect days. It's okay to not always be on top of Motivation Mountain.

Most people think this positive characteristic is [Y]:

We tend to think of motivation as a tireless source of driving intrinsic energy and we get confused when we lose it, when we feel unmotivated.

When it's really [x]:

But motivation is not a sprint, it's a marathon. It's not giving up on trying to have perfect days.

We *hired* a new employee yesterday.

And he already created a problem for us.

He's remote. He's young.

And ambitious.

He took part of my co-founder's job in the first three hours.

Didn't even ask him.

He saw an area for improvement, then just did it.

We gave him a stepping stone.

Part-time this month working remote.

And he took the small opportunity to get noticed.

As a startup, it's hard to hire remote workers.

You're building your core team.

The team to lead hundreds of employees one day.

The worst thing I can do is look at all the traditional reasons not to hire him.

The best thing —
Look at his motivation, skill set, and values.

And the fact that he's been following our company for almost a year.

That's not written on his resume.

These are the intangibles.

I'm not perfect at hiring.

I let three people go in our first three months.

But I'm improving.

That's why today I lend my hand in areas where I once hesitated.

As the CEO, it's my responsibility to vouch for them.

Then provide a window to see their potential.

No matter how small.

I don't care if you're remote.

A minority.

Over 50.

Young.

Value is only seen once given an opportunity.

Only then can you measure persistence.

And ambition.

— We made a decision recently to work with someone: —

*We **hired** a new employee yesterday.*

— It's become a problem: —

And he already created a problem for us.

— For these controversial reasons: —

He's remote. He's young. And ambitious.

— Then they did this out-of-line action: —

He took part of my co-founder's job in the first three hours. Didn't even ask him.

— But they did it to provide value: —

He saw an area for improvement, then just did it.

We gave them a chance:

We gave him a stepping stone. Part-time this month working remote.

They took it as an opportunity:

And he took the small opportunity to get noticed.

It's not easy taking chances in our position:

As a startup, it's hard to hire remote workers.

For this reason that will lead to this larger tangible result:

You're building your core team. The team to lead hundreds of employees one day.

I didn't focus on vanity:

The worst thing I can do is look at all the traditional reasons not to hire him. The best thing —

Instead, I focused on defining characteristics:

Look at his motivation, skill set, and values.
And the fact that he's been following our company for almost a year.

You won't find these characteristics in the traditional area:

That's not written on his resume. These are the intangibles.

I'm not a saint:

I'm not perfect at hiring.

Here's a tangible example:

I let three people go in our first three months.

I'm getting better:

But I'm improving.

┌─ That's why today I can help where I once couldn't: ─┐

That's why today I lend my hand in areas where I once hesitated.

├─ It's my responsibility to give them a chance: ─

As the CEO, it's my responsibility to vouch for them. Then provide a window to see their potential. No matter how small.

├─ It doesn't matter if they have these qualities: ─

I don't care if you're remote. A minority. Over 50. Young.

├─ The learning lesson: ─

Value is only seen once given an opportunity. Only then can you measure persistence. And ambition.

A young woman messaged me on LinkedIn.

She wanted career advice.

We met in a cafe.

She said, "I'm at a crossroads. I want to found a company, but I have an offer to work in real estate."

I replied, "What are the benefits of each?"

"People tell me I'd be great at real estate."

I stopped her.

And told her a story.

When I started writing, all my friends and family laughed for years.

I don't blame them. I was an awful writer.

They said,

"You should get into finance."

"You should study law."

I refused every time.

Even when I published my first book, they didn't take me seriously.

It took five years, thousands of articles, and three books before I developed a loyal audience.

And earned their respect.

It was worth it.

Because I loved writing.

I wouldn't trade it for anything in the world.

I then said, "What you believe you can become is far different than what others believe. The best thing you can do is trust yourself first.

What does your gut say you want to do with your life?"

She didn't respond.

But we both knew the answer.

It's not my job to tell her what route to pick.

Nor is it the job of her family and friends.

It's her choice.

She already knew the right decision.

I didn't do anything special.

I just reminded her.

— Someone reached out for help: —

A young woman messaged me on LinkedIn. She wanted career advice.

— We met in a nice place: —

We met in a cafe.

— They told me their problem: —

She said, "I'm at a crossroads. I want to found a company, but I have an offer to work in real estate."

— I asked a simple question: —

I replied, "What are the benefits of each?"

— They gave an inadequate response: —

"People tell me I'd be great at real estate."

I cut them off to tell them a relevant story:

I stopped her. And told her a story.

No one believed in what I wanted to do:

When I started writing, all my friends and family laughed for years.

It's not their fault:

I don't blame them. I was an awful writer.

They told me to do something different:

They said, "You should get into finance." "You should study law."

I never gave up:

I refused every time.

Even when I expected their appreciation, they didn't give it:

Even when I published my first book, they didn't take me seriously.

It's only when I did all of this — did they respect me:

It took five years, thousands of articles, and three books before I developed a loyal audience. And earned their respect.

It worked out:

It was worth it. Because I loved writing.
I wouldn't trade it for anything in the world.

So I asked them a question related to the learning lesson of the story:

I then said, "What you believe you can become is far different than what others believe. The best thing you can do is trust yourself first. What does your gut say you want to do with your life?"

— They didn't need to respond: ─────────────

She didn't respond. But we both knew the answer.

— It's not my job to give advice nor anyone else's: ─────

It's not my job to tell her what route to pick. Nor is it the job of her family and friends.

— It's up to the person to choose their route: ─────

It's her choice. She already knew the right decision.

— I reminded them of that fact: ─────────

I didn't do anything special. I just reminded her.

BEING RECOGNIZED BY BRILLIANT PEOPLE

Yesterday, I was on a phone call with a founder of a billion-dollar company.

He was interested in having us manage his personal brand.

He talked about his story of being homeless and collecting cans to leading a company that employed 10,000 people.

Knowing the rarity of such a conversation, I listened to every word.

He said, "Josh, you sound like someone who knows what they're doing."

I replied, "It's not me. The truth is I have a brilliant team."

He laughed, "You just proved my point."

I thought about that conversation all today.

As I've stepped into leadership shoes, I've realized how important it is to hire people smarter than you.

Everyone around me knows more about their niche than I do.

It makes me more confident in my company, BAMF Media, than ever.

And it's humbling.

I get to feel like a kid who learns something new every day.

If you can put enough smart friends in a room together, then you have unlimited potential.

Most entrepreneurs forget this.

They look at entrepreneurship as a lonely journey.

I did this, too.

It's not.

The key to entrepreneurship is building relationships.

Surround yourself with people smarter than you.

If you like each other, it's even better.

If you can agree on an idea —
Then you have a company.

I had a high-stakes meeting with an important individual:

Yesterday, I was on a phone call with a founder of a billion-dollar company.

They needed an important job done:

He was interested in having us manage his personal brand.

They explained their hero's journey story:

He talked about his story of being homeless and collecting cans to leading a company that employed 10,000 people.

I took the opportunity seriously:

Knowing the rarity of such a conversation, I listened to every word.

They expressed a statement of praise:

He said, "Josh, you sound like someone who knows what they're doing."

I said the praise is better for my team:

I replied, "It's not me. The truth is I have a brilliant team."

This proved their point:

He laughed, "You just proved my point."

The conversation resonated with me for a reason that ties into my praise:

I thought about that conversation all today. As I've stepped into leadership shoes, I've realized how important it is to hire people smarter than you.

That is why I'm surrounded by great people:

Everyone around me knows more about their niche than I do.

It provides this benefit to what we're working on:

It makes me more confident in my company, BAMF Media, than ever. And it's humbling.

It's the best feeling with this metaphor:

I get to feel like a kid who learns something new every day.

Here's the overarching learning lesson:

If you can put enough smart friends in a room together, then you have unlimited potential.

Some people forget this and see it in this negative way:

Most entrepreneurs forget this. They look at entrepreneurship as a lonely journey.

I was once there:

I did this, too. It's not.

Here's the real secret — it's the opposite:

The key to entrepreneurship is building relationships.
Surround yourself with people smarter than you.
If you like each other, it's even better.
If you can agree on an idea —

The positive result:

Then you have a company.

TAKE ADVANTAGE
OF MORE OPPORTUNITIES

Last night, I took a flight to South Korea.

I sat next to an older Filipino lady.

Rarely do I talk to the passengers I sit next to on a plane.

I'm too shy to make an introduction.

She turned to me with a wide smile, "What's your name?"

I said, "Josh."

This small moment led to several hours of conversation.

She talked about her passion to rebuild broken communities.

And about the Filipino culture.

Then she said, "My husband and I have been adopting runaways from broken homes for the last ten years."

It's inspiring.

She's held to a wheelchair and has more energy than I do.

I asked her what keeps her motivated.

"I surround myself with people who laugh often."

Right before we departed, we exchanged contact information.

With kind eyes, she said, "When you're back in Los Angeles, come visit my family for dinner."

This small exchange made me ashamed at every time I've taken a plane and didn't introduce myself.

It all started with a simple line,

"What's your name?"

That's how easy it is to open yourself up to a new learning experience.

Yet, so many of us don't do this.

The key to growth is listening.

We often forget the best opportunities to listen are all around us.

Whether on a plane, bus, or even an Uber ride.

Next time, I'll say "Hi."

I made a big life change:

Last night, I took a flight to South Korea.

Next to this person:

I sat next to an older Filipino lady.

— I don't normally meet people in this type of life change:

Rarely do I talk to the passengers I sit next to on a plane.

— Because I have this "innocent" quality:

I'm too shy to make an introduction.

— They introduced themselves to me:

She turned to me with a wide smile, "What's your name?" I said, "Josh."

— This led to something unexpected:

This small moment led to several hours of conversation.

— They told their incredible story:

She talked about her passion to rebuild broken communities. And about the Filipino culture.
Then she said, "My husband and I have been adopting runaways from broken homes for the last ten years." It's inspiring.

— They surprised me because they had this obstacle to — overcome:

She's held to a wheelchair and has more energy than I do.

— I asked them what's the difference: —

I asked her what keeps her motivated.
"I surround myself with people who laugh often."

— I made sure to keep in touch: —

Right before we departed, we exchanged contact information.

— They gave a reason to continue conversation at a — later date:

With kind eyes, she said, "When you're back in Los Angeles, come visit my family for dinner."

— This made me feel bad for this common action I've — taken:

This small exchange made me ashamed at every time I've taken a plane and didn't introduce myself.

— It all comes down to this one question: —

It all started with a simple line, "What's your name?"

— That's all it takes to get this benefit: —

That's how easy it is to open yourself up to a new learning experience.

— The majority doesn't do it: —

Yet, so many of us don't do this.

— The realization: —

The key to growth is listening.

— How it ties into the learning lesson of the story: —

We often forget the best opportunities to listen are all around us.

— A tangible way to use the learning lesson: —

Whether on a plane, bus, or even an Uber ride. Next time, I'll say "Hi."

I took a sales call at 2 a.m.

Then slept for an hour before another sales call at 4 a.m.

As January approaches, companies are choosing their vendors.

We're in go mode.

This means working with international prospects when they work.

As the CEO, I make time.

If it means napping between calls, then so be it.

If you want to compete with the best, you have to be willing to do what they're not.

And more.

In December, when our competitors are sleeping —
We're hopping on video calls.

Designing proposals.

Sending emails.

You can't have the word BAMF in your company name, then put out average work.

We take pride in what we represent.

Not by words.

By action.

This attitude took us from 0 - 2 million in annual revenue in six months with zero client churn.

If you want to set yourself apart, then stop copying your competitors.

And take action where they're afraid to.

December is not peacetime.

It's wartime.

Strap your vest on, then get in the trenches.

If you want to be first on your prospect's list —
Do things that don't scale.

And do them well.

┌─ I went above and beyond with hustle: ──────────
I took a sales call at 2 a.m.

├─ Then hustled even harder: ──────────
Then slept for an hour before another sales call at 4 a.m.

For this reason:

*As January approaches, companies are choosing their vendors.
We're in go mode.*

That's why I take this above and beyond action:

This means working with international prospects when they work.

It's my job to make it happen:

As the CEO, I make time.

Even if I suffer this amount:

If it means napping between calls, then so be it.

Because here's what I learned:

*If you want to compete with the best, you have to be willing to do what they're
not. And more.*

When people aren't taking action:

In December, when our competitors are sleeping —

We're taking action with these specific steps:

We're hopping on video calls. Designing proposals. Sending emails.

It's for our brand:

You can't have the word BAMF in your company name, then put out average work. We take pride in what we represent. Not by words. By action.

Here are the positive results of this mentality:

This attitude took us from 0 - 2 million in annual revenue in six months with zero client churn.

The learning lesson:

If you want to set yourself apart, then stop copying your competitors. And take action where they're afraid to.

Time is better now than ever:

December is not peacetime. It's wartime.

So here's a metaphor of taking action:

Strap your vest on, then get in the trenches.

To get this positive result:

If you want to be first on your prospect's list —

Take this counterintuitive advice:

Do things that don't scale. And do them well.

CHOOSE VALUE OVER VANITY

The night before I left Thailand, I had dinner with a woman I met online.

She owns one of the largest luxury hotel chains.

Sitting at the table was also an Instagram influencer with over 12 million followers.

The woman didn't know much about social media.

She wanted to learn about it from us.

I said, "It's no different than in-person communication. It's when people think it's different — is when they lose."

She responded, "Why is that?"

"We all build rapport the same way whether online or offline. If you want to make a strong connection, you need quality communication."

"That's so refreshing to hear."

Many people are scared to use social media because they think it's vanity driven. It's true.

Here's the problem: The vanity doesn't get results.

No real relationships get built.

It's the people who share genuine stories who see the benefit.

Because people don't buy things, they buy the journey behind them.

And the tools will always change.

Friendster no longer exists.

Same with MySpace.

And Vine.

The stories stayed.

They just moved to another platform.

That's why it doesn't matter if you have the latest tech.

It's only an amplifier.

You win with genuine communication.

By simply being you.

I met this person from a controversial setting:

The night before I left Thailand, I had dinner with a woman I met online.

They had a lot of credibility:

She owns one of the largest luxury hotel chains.

This credible person was also there:

Sitting at the table was also an Instagram influencer with over 12 million followers.

First person had a problem:

The woman didn't know much about social media.

They wanted us to solve it:

She wanted to learn about it from us.

I told them they already have the skills:

I said, "It's no different than in-person communication. It's when people think it's different — is when they lose."

They asked why that's true:

She responded, "Why is that?"

I broke it down in a simple way:

"We all build rapport the same way whether online or offline. If you want to make a strong connection, you need quality communication."

They expressed happiness about it:

"That's so refreshing to hear."

Here's the overarching problem:

Many people are scared to use social media because they think it's vanity driven. It's true.

Here's the problem boiled down:

Here's the problem: The vanity doesn't get results.

Tie the problem back to #8:

No real relationships get built.

— This is what people should do instead: —

It's the people who share genuine stories who see the benefit.

— For this reason: —

Because people don't buy things, they buy the journey behind them.

— Remember these negative events: —

And the tools will always change. Friendster no longer exists. Same with MySpace. And Vine.

— Tie #15 into #14: —

The stories stayed. They just moved to another platform.

— The realization: —

That's why it doesn't matter if you have the latest tech. It's only an amplifier.

— The learning lesson: —

You win with genuine communication. By simply being you.

PERFECT TIMING

My employee asked, "How much time do I have off for the holidays?"

I replied, "As much time as you want."

I don't micromanage.

Instead, I hire people I trust.

Because I didn't found BAMF Media to provide daycare services.

I founded it to give people the creative freedom they've always wanted.

And if I hire people who respect this culture, they'll make the right decisions.

Agree?

Person asks you a vulnerable question about something that's happening for many people (e.g. Christmas):

My employee asked, "How much time do I have off for the holidays?"

You reply in the most positive way:

I replied, "As much time as you want."

— I don't take this negative action: —————————

I don't micromanage.

— I do it the right way: ——————————

Instead, I hire people I trust.

— For this reason with this metaphor: —————

Because I didn't found BAMF Media to provide daycare services.

— Here's an expanded reason: ——————

I founded it to give people the creative freedom they've always wanted.

— If I do it this way, then it will work out: —————

And if I hire people who respect this culture, they'll make the right decisions. Agree?

My first employee is an immigrant.

He got rejected by Facebook, Snapchat, and Google.

They didn't want to deal with visa issues.

I knew we were taking a risk hiring him. I just didn't know how valuable he'd become.

And now he might get deported.

All I want for the holidays are better immigration laws.

He studied at Berkeley for 4 years, worked for notable tech companies, and helped us grow to a company of sixteen.

It doesn't matter.

The immigration system says "he's not worthy" to participate here.

Many people like our employee, Hendry, sacrificed everything to move to the U.S. to build their career.

They have an American Dream.

The government is taking it away.

They don't care how much value he adds.

But we care.

So even if they deport him, we'll still work with him.

Because 2018 doesn't recognize borders.

We're here to prove it.

A controversial characteristic about someone close to you:
My first employee is an immigrant.

They went through this hard time with big brand names because of it:
He got rejected by Facebook, Snapchat, and Google.
They didn't want to deal with visa issues.

I took a risk to associate with them not knowing how close we'd become:
I knew we were taking a risk hiring him. I just didn't know how valuable he'd become.

Now the worst thing might happen to them:
And now he might get deported.

— For this relevant situation most of us our in (e.g.
holidays), I want this to get fixed:

All I want for the holidays are better immigration laws.

— They've accomplished so much:

He studied at Berkeley for 4 years, worked for notable tech companies, and helped us grow to a company of sixteen. It doesn't matter.

— But that's not what the broken system says:

The immigration system says "he's not worthy" to participate here.

— Even though they did everything they could:

Many people like our employee, Hendry, sacrificed everything to move to the U.S. to build their career.

— They have this important commonality we all share:

They have an American Dream.

It's been ripped away by this evil thing:

The government is taking it away. They don't care how much value he adds.

We'll stand up for them:

But we care.

No matter what:

So even if they deport him, we'll still work with him.

For this controversial reason:

Because 2018 doesn't recognize borders. We're here to prove it.

MAKE EXCEPTIONS
FOR EXCEPTIONAL PEOPLE

My employee didn't haven't anyone to celebrate Christmas with.

He's a 21-year-old army veteran.

He just flew in from Chicago.

I spent the day with him.

He's staying at my place while he finds housing.

We ate Chinese food, listened to music, and watched funny videos.

He didn't come from any fancy school.

He never graduated college.

The first time I met him, he drove an hour and a half to see me speak.

I was impressed with his understanding of marketing technology.

And that he had founded an agency.

He said, "I want to work for you."

I replied, "I'll see what I can do."

Two weeks later, we started him on contract working remote.

A month later, he was on calls with $200K prospects.

At only twenty one, Arri is already making an impact.

His route?

Untraditional.

His attitude?

The difference maker.

We hired him.

He didn't have a place.

So we gave him one.

When you have exceptional people—you make exceptions.

A problem of someone close to you that many people can resonate with:

My employee didn't haven't anyone to celebrate Christmas with.

They're a minority:

He's a 21-year-old army veteran.

— Taking a chance: ————————————————————

He just flew in from Chicago.

— I solved their problem by doing this: ——————

I spent the day with him.
He's staying at my place while he finds housing.
We ate Chinese food, listened to music, and watched funny videos.

— They didn't have these prestigious qualities: ————

He didn't come from any fancy school. He never graduated college.

— It didn't matter because they took these positive ——
actions:

The first time I met him, he drove an hour and a half to see me speak.
I was impressed with his understanding of marketing technology.
And that he had founded an agency.

— They told me they wanted to join what I created: —

He said, "I want to work for you." I replied, "I'll see what I can do."

— I gave them a small chance: —

Two weeks later, we started him on contract working remote.

— They exceeded expectations: —

A month later, he was on calls with $200K prospects.

— Even with this obstacle: —

At only twenty one, Arri is already making an impact.

— They had these polar opposite attributes: —

His route? Untraditional. His attitude? The difference maker.

— We brought them into what I created: —

We hired him.

— Giving them what they were missing: ——————

He didn't have a place. So we gave him one.

— This is the learning lesson: ——————————————

When you have exceptional people — you make exceptions.

FUNNY SET-BY-STEP TO ACCOMPLISH A GOAL

How I founded a multi-million-dollar agency in six months:

Step 1: Quit job.

Step 2: Move cities.

Step 3: Go out drinking with a new friend.

Step 4: After several hours of knowing them, invest all your money into their idea.

Step 5: Purchase an office you can't afford.

Step 6: Call your parents saying, "I made a huge mistake."

Step 7: Land one client who barely covers rent. And keep paying yourself nothing.

Step 8: Make sure to drink all the free beer in the coworking space to survive.

Step 9: Turn the client into a believer who refers two more clients.

Step 10: Hire your first paid intern.

Step 11: Change everything about the business.

Step 12: Realize that nothing you do is certain to work out.

Step 13: Something works out.

Step 14: Double down on it.

Step 15: Profit.

Step 16: Write viral rags to riches LinkedIn posts.

Step 17: Call your parents saying, "I'm a genius."

Step 18: Learn to ignore the haters.

— How I accomplished this huge goal: ——

How I founded a multi-million-dollar agency in six months:

— Took a risk: ——

Step 1: Quit job.

— Took another risk: ——

Step 2: Move cities.

— Did something to hurt my sense of judgment: ——

Step 3: Go out drinking with a new friend.

— That led to taking a crazy risk: ——

Step 4: After several hours of knowing them, invest all your money into their idea.

Then I took another risk:

Step 5: Purchase an office you can't afford.

Had to admit it to people I cared about:

Step 6: Call your parents saying, "I made a huge mistake."

Then I saw hope, but my circumstances didn't improve much:

Step 7: Land one client who barely covers rent. And keep paying yourself nothing.

I took advantage of all the small benefits of my situation:

Step 8: Make sure to drink all the free beer in the coworking space to survive.

Then made the most out of the hope:

Step 9: Turn the client into a believer who refers two more clients.

Made a big step in progress:

Step 10: Hire your first paid intern.

Decided to do everything differently:

Step 11: Change everything about the business.

Came to a funny realization:

Step 12: Realize that nothing you do is certain to work out.

That had an ironic twist:

Step 13: Something works out.

So I put all my chips down:

Step 14: Double down on it.

Got a great result:

Step 15: Profit.

So I take these funny and ironic steps now:

Step 16: Write viral rags to riches LinkedIn posts.
Step 17: Call your parents saying, "I'm a genius."
Step 18: Learn to ignore the haters.

CHANGE YOUR MIND
NOT THEIRS

I was on a call yesterday with a prospect. He wanted a discount.

He said, "I want you to earn my business."

I replied, "It's a two-way street."

When I founded my company, I'd do anything to land a client.

We gave lots of discounts.

The result? Low margins.

Clients who always wanted more.

Asking for a discount says, "I don't trust you to deliver."

Rather than getting upset at prospects, I flipped it around.

I asked, "How can we build more trust?"

We wrote two books.

Published more blog posts.

Did more speaking engagements.

And you know what happened? They still asked for discounts.

This time we were prepared.

All that trust building gave us more prospects.

It gave us the confidence to say "no."

What I realized?

You can't always change the mind of your prospects.

But you sure can change yours.

I had a recent event where someone told me I wasn't worth it:

I was on a call yesterday with a prospect. He wanted a discount.

They said this statement devaluing my work:

He said, "I want you to earn my business."

I said it works both ways with a metaphor:

I replied, "It's a two-way street."

I remember when it wasn't always like this:

When I founded my company, I'd do anything to land a client.

We gave into people's demands:

We gave lots of discounts.

It turned out ugly:

The result? Low margins. Clients who always wanted more.
Asking for a discount says, "I don't trust you to deliver."

Instead of getting angry, I looked for a solution:

Rather than getting upset at prospects, I flipped it around.
I asked, "How can we build more trust?"

Then created that solution:

We wrote two books. Published more blog posts.
Did more speaking engagements.

As a result, it didn't change how they approached me:

And you know what happened? They still asked for discounts.

I had leverage now because of a key action:

This time we were prepared. All that trust building gave us more prospects. It gave us the confidence to say "no."

Here's the learning lesson:

What I realized? You can't always change the mind of your prospects. But you sure can change yours.

GET PEOPLE TO DEMAND WHAT YOU'RE WORTH

I interviewed an entrepreneur who sold his company for 50 million dollars to Walmart. Here's what happened:

Me: "When you found out Walmart didn't want to acquire you, what did you do next?"

Fraser: "We continued working on the company, and eventually Amazon approached us."

Me: "Oh wow. Amazon."

Fraser: "As soon as Walmart found out about Amazon, they offered to acquire us."

When people perceive you're in high demand, then they'll chase after you.

I've used this tactic by interviewing with two companies that are direct competitors. This moves you through the interview process faster.

I've also used this tactic when a hiring manager asks me what my timeline looks like to start the job.

"It can be in a week or two months. I have a few founders who want to do projects with me. Let me know what works best for you."

If you said you had nothing happening, then that shows a low demand for you.

The lesson: encourage people to compete for your time.

You'll get better opportunities faster.

I talked to someone who had a huge accomplishment:

I interviewed an entrepreneur who sold his company for 50 million dollars to Walmart. Here's what happened:

I asked them about the negative situation it started in:

Me: "When you found out Walmart didn't want to acquire you, what did you do next?"

They told us how it turned into a positive:

Fraser: "We continued working on the company, and eventually Amazon approached us." Me: "Oh wow. Amazon."

Then how that positive turned into a bigger one:

Fraser: "As soon as Walmart found out about Amazon, they offered to acquire us."

Here's the learning lesson:

When people perceive you're in high demand, then they'll chase after you.

I've used this learning lesson before in these situations with this tangible example:

I've used this tactic by interviewing with two companies that are direct competitors. This moves you through the interview process faster. I've also used this tactic when a hiring manager asks me what my timeline looks like to start the job. "It can be in a week or two months. I have a few founders who want to do projects with me. Let me know what works best for you."

Here's why I used it:

If you said you had nothing happening, then that shows a low demand for you.

Here's the primary lesson reiterated in other words:

The lesson: encourage people to compete for your time.
You'll get better opportunities faster.

I hired a 21-year-old immigrant without a college degree.

I turned down Stanford and USC graduates for the same position.

As a dropout, no one wanted to hire him.

His parents told him, "being an immigrant with no degree is the last position you want to be in — in this country."

Rather than take a marketing 101 course, he left college and took an online Messenger marketing course.

It's one of the hottest skills in-demand today.

To keep a roof over his head, he drove Uber every week.

Several times over, he ran out of savings.

Still, he kept grinding.

Then landed a few clients.

We tested him out.

After a day, we knew we'd hire him.

As a business, we don't run like a charity.

We hire people who will give us the highest R.O.I.

The best part?

He proves there's more than one way to become successful.

You don't need Stanford, Berkeley, or Harvard on your resume.

You don't even need college.

Because at the age of 21 —
Arri has a well-paying job.

No debt.

And the brightest future ahead of him.

— **I gave this person a chance even with this** —
controversial background:
I hired a 21-year-old immigrant without a college degree.

— **I turned down these people with traditionally more** —
qualified backgrounds:
I turned down Stanford and USC graduates for the same position.

— **No one gave them a chance:** —
As a dropout, no one wanted to hire him.

Not even the people who care about them:

His parents told him, "being an immigrant with no degree is the last position you want to be in — in this country."

They didn't listen — and hustled:

Rather than take a marketing 101 course, he left college and took an online Messenger marketing course. It's one of the hottest skills in-demand today.

Hustled even more:

To keep a roof over his head, he drove Uber every week.

It didn't always work out:

Several times over, he ran out of savings.

They kept going and had some success:

Still, he kept grinding. Then landed a few clients.

So we gave them a window of opportunity:

We tested him out.

They exceeded expectations:

After a day, we knew we'd hire him.

It's not our position to do favors:

As a business, we don't run like a charity.

We just see people differently:

We hire people who will give us the highest R.O.I.

Here's what we learned:

The best part? He proves there's more than one way to become successful.

You don't need traditional ways of success:

You don't need Stanford, Berkeley, or Harvard on your resume.
You don't even need college.

They're proof of it:

Because at the age of 21 — Arri has a well-paying job. No debt.
And the brightest future ahead of him.

BEING RIGHT DOESN'T MATTER

We had a three-month contract with a client.

Then broke it.

My co-founder, Houston, wanted to honor it.

"He signed for three months. And we're doing good work."

The client didn't care.

His timeline had changed for the project.

He wanted out.

We hopped on a phone call.

Tempers flared.

Accusations were made.

We looked at each other and remembered a core company principle,

"Kill them with kindness."

Time wasted arguing is time wasted not getting results.

He agreed.

We let the client out of the contract.

For one reason: we have an abundant mindset.

The hard reality is you won't get along with every client.

And it's better to move on faster.

But moving on requires you to look at new opportunities.

Not chasing what could've been with lawyers.

After the conversation ended, I said, "let's send out a hundred emails to leads in the next thirty minutes."

The result?

I woke up this morning with five replies from prospects interested in working with us.

It's a reminder,
A reminder that no contract is perfect for every situation.

That time is your most precious asset.

That being right doesn't matter.

Because when you no longer accept mediocrity —
Fear of loss disappears.

And you're left taking the most important step —
One forward.

We ended a relationship with someone close to us:

We had a three-month contract with a client. Then broke it.

We almost didn't:

My co-founder, Houston, wanted to honor it.
"He signed for three months. And we're doing good work."

The problem:

The client didn't care. His timeline had changed for the project.
He wanted out.

We tried to resolve the issue with the person:

We hopped on a phone call.

It only got worse:

Tempers flared. Accusations were made.

Then we remembered this important value:

We looked at each other and remembered a core company principle,
"Kill them with kindness."

This means:

Time wasted arguing is time wasted not getting results. He agreed.

So we ended the relationship for this reason:

We let the client out of the contract.
For one reason: we have an abundant mindset.

It's not easy, but here's what you can do about it:

The hard reality is you won't get along with every client.
And it's better to move on faster.

Take a positive perspective on it:

But moving on requires you to look at new opportunities.
Not chasing what could've been with lawyers.

Then we took a positive action:

After the conversation ended, I said, "let's send out a hundred emails to leads in the next thirty minutes." The result?

Got positive results:

I woke up this morning with five replies from prospects interested in working with us.

Here's how it shows the bigger, positive picture with these learning lessons:

It's a reminder, A reminder that no contract is perfect for every situation. That time is your most precious asset. That being right doesn't matter.

For this reason:

Because when you no longer accept mediocrity — Fear of loss disappears.

So you achieve this positive result:

And you're left taking the most important step — One forward.

LEADERSHIP IS A CHOICE

It's intimidating.

As a 26-year-old CEO, most of my employees are older than me.

And I never asked for their respect.

I earned it.

I went through 8 failed startups as a founder and marketer.

Built a community of 17,000 founders and marketers.

Wrote four technical marketing books.

After my early failures, I've led growth at several successful companies.

And I used my community to grow over one thousand companies in 2017.

I get thank-you messages every day.

And still, "well-respected" people in the industry tell me I haven't "earned" it.

As a young founder, I've learned the only respect I need to earn is that of my employees and my own.

People will always find a reason to knock you, especially if they're jealous.

Let them focus on you.

Then ignore them to focus on the people you've hired.

Because they need you for their families, job security, and to have a mission that gives them purpose.

And never forget — your age doesn't matter.

Leadership is a choice.

A choice to feel the fear, then take the first step anyways.

An emotional obstacle:

It's intimidating.

As someone X years old in Y position, I face this controversial situation:

As a 26-year-old CEO, most of my employees are older than me.

I don't act needy:

And I never asked for their respect. I earned it.

I paid my dues with these tangible experiences:

I went through 8 failed startups as a founder and marketer.
Built a community of 17,000 founders and marketers.
Wrote four technical marketing books.

I even climbed this far up the ladder:

After my early failures, I've led growth at several successful companies.

Then made this huge accomplishment:

And I used my community to grow over one thousand companies in 2017.

It comes with recognition:

I get thank-you messages every day.

But there's always hate with these tangible examples:

And still, "well-respected" people in the industry tell me I haven't "earned" it

I know better than to give in:

As a young founder, I've learned the only respect I need to earn is that of my employees and my own.

There will always be the negative:

People will always find a reason to knock you, especially if they're jealous.

Don't worry about it — focus on moving forward:

Let them focus on you. Then ignore them to concentrate on the people you've hired.

You got people depending on you:

Because they need you for their families, job security, and to have a mission that gives them purpose.

Don't let your vulnerabilities hold you back:

And never forget — your age doesn't matter.

Anyone can be great:

Leadership is a choice. A choice to feel the fear, then take the first step anyways.

THE BEST INSIST ON TAKING ACTION

This week, we hired a senior marketer.

He insisted he take part in our $200,000 deal negotiation.

And crushed it.

I can't afford people who are content with clocking in 9 – 5.

People who work a job because it's just that — a job.

"You don't do that in your first week."

"It's not even why we hired you."

"You need to earn it."

Don't believe it.

You do what helps the company grow.

Not just your job description.

If we all followed guidelines, then we'd never improve.

We hire people with a growth mindset.

Willing to step on toes.

Willing to place their foot down and say, "Bring me to the table"

Every employee is a salesperson.

And a problem solver.

The best ones?

They insist on it.

Welcome to the team, Charles.

We brought an experienced person onto our team:

This week, we hired a senior marketer.

He demanded a larger role:

He insisted he take part in our $200,000 deal negotiation.

Then succeeded:

And crushed it.

I don't want people who don't want to level up:

I can't afford people who are content with clocking in 9 – 5.
People who work a job because it's just that — a job.

Here are some examples of negative feedback people get when demanding a larger role:

"You don't do that in your first week." "It's not even why we hired you." "You need to earn it." Don't believe it.

Focus on growth over everything else:

You do what helps the company grow. Not just your job description.

Break the rules to grow:

If we all followed guidelines, then we'd never improve.

These are the type of people we add to our team:

We hire people with a growth mindset. Willing to step on toes. Willing to place their foot down and say, "Bring me to the table"

Here's why:

Every employee is a salesperson. And a problem solver.

And most importantly, they do X [tie back to the beginning]:

The best ones? They insist on it. Welcome to the team, Charles.

STAND FOR SOMETHING

2018 doesn't recognize borders.

I can hire and scale a remote team of hundreds of workers.

I can serve thousands of clients.

While never leaving my room.

We employ people in the Philippines, Indonesia, Florida, Chicago, San Francisco, South Africa, Morocco, and Thailand.

It's not about how many people are on your team.

It's about who's on your team.

If I want to hire the best—I don't care where they live.
I care about results.

Even if the law passes to curb H-1B visa extensions resulting in 500,000+ deportations—we'll still hire you.

Because in 2018, great work doesn't recognize borders.

It recognizes people.

Start with a controversial statement:

2018 doesn't recognize borders.

Explain why it's true:

I can hire and scale a remote team of hundreds of workers.
I can serve thousands of clients.

All with less work:

While never leaving my room.

Make it more tangible:

We employ people in the Philippines, Indonesia, Florida, Chicago, San Francisco, South Africa, Morocco, and Thailand.

It's quality over quantity:

It's not about how many people are on your team. It's about who's on your team.

No matter what:

If I want to hire the best — I don't care where they live.

At the end of the day, this is what matters: ——————

I care about results.

Even if this new popular and controversial event ——— happens:

Even if the law passes to curb H-1B visa extensions resulting in 500,000+ deportations — we'll still hire you.

Tie the reason back to the beginning, then humanize ——— it:

Because in 2018, great work doesn't recognize borders. It recognizes people.

PREPARE BY TAKING ACTION

I sent four offer letters last night.

Two accepted this morning.

I'm not perfect.

We let go of our first three employees.

But we learned.

So we only let go one of our last twenty.

And here I am eight months later with almost twenty-six employees at BAMF Media.

The funny part?

It's my twelfth try at startup success.

I worked for eight startups that failed. And three that did okay.

That's brutal odds.

The reason I'm more successful today is simple: Practice. Over and over again.

I practiced every day for five years being a better entrepreneur.

That meant I had to learn all of this:
> How to make sales
> Find a co-founder
> Hire employees
> Fire employees

> › Market my company
> › Work with a lawyer
> › Work with a CFO
> › Create a service customers love
> › Price services
> › Understand business analytics
> › Motivate employees
> › Create a community

That's a ton of lessons.

And why it can take a long time to found a successful company.

Here's the twist: Every learning lesson above requires you to practice entrepreneurship.

So if you want to know the best way to prepare yourself — jump right in.

I wanted to add a lot of people to my team:

I sent four offer letters last night.

It worked out well:

Two accepted this morning.

It wasn't always this easy:

I'm not perfect. We let go of our first three employees.

We improved with this tangible example:

But we learned. So we only let go one of our last twenty.

As a result, we've had success:

And here I am eight months later with almost twenty-six employees at BAMF Media.

It's ironic for these reasons:

The funny part? It's my twelfth try at startup success. I worked for eight startups that failed. And three that did okay.

That's why it's hard:

That's brutal odds.

It worked out because I put in the work:

The reason I'm more successful today is simple: practice. Over and over again. I practiced every day for five years being a better entrepreneur.

That meant I had to do all of these things:

That meant I had to learn all of this: - How to make sales - Find a co-founder - Hire employees - Fire employees - Market my company - Work with a lawyer - Work with a CFO - Create a service customers love - Price services - Understand business analytics - Motivate employees - Create a community That's a ton of lessons.

That's why few can do it:

And why it can take a long time to found a successful company.

Here's the truth about learning - you need to take action:

Here's the twist: Every learning lesson above requires you to practice entrepreneurship.
So if you want to know the best way to prepare yourself — jump right in.

CAN'T CONTROL WHAT HAPPENS TO YOU

Yesterday, I heard a knock on my hotel door.

A staff member stood there.

"You have ten minutes to one."

"Do I need to check out or something?"

"Yes."

I thought, "Shoot — I have a video call with a prospect at one."

Not just with one person, but an entire C-level team.
I asked myself, "What are the solutions here?"

...."Hotel lobby."

I rush to pack up everything in 30 seconds.

I go down to the lobby and check out while looking at my phone.

2 minutes till the meeting.

I sit on one of the empty couches.

Flip open my laptop.

Then I hear a hundred footsteps walk through the door.

It's a group getting off a charter bus for a conference.

I'm hopelessly praying that they'll be quiet.

Then I hear a thunder of rattling.

A construction noise a couple of floors below.

Before I can find a solution the screens changes.

They're there.

The CEO, CMO, and right-hand executives.

And I'm in the middle of Jumanji.

For forty-five minutes I present.

I'm at 150% confidence the entire time.

Here's what I do know: You can't always control what happens to you.

So I apply a five-minute rule.

I allow myself to be upset for 5 minutes.

That's it.

Because I got a lot of years ahead of me to close deals.

And the biggest ones you lose today?

Will be the smallest in the long run.

Recently I had to leave my setting ASAP:

Yesterday, I heard a knock on my hotel door. A staff member stood there. "You have ten minutes to one." "Do I need to check out or something?" "Yes."

Here's the problem - I had a lot on the line:

I thought, "Shoot — I have a video call with a prospect at one." Not just with one person, but an entire C-level team.

I figured out a solution:

I asked myself, "What are the solutions here?" ...."Hotel lobby."

Then made it happen:

I rush to pack up everything in 30 seconds. I go down to the lobby and check out while looking at my phone. 2 minutes till the meeting. I sit on one of the empty couches. Flip open my laptop.

Then trouble ensues right when the solution is put in place:

Then I hear a hundred footsteps walk through the door. It's a group getting off a charter bus for a conference. I'm hopelessly praying that they'll be quiet. Then I hear a thunder of rattling. A construction noise a couple of floors below.

I can't fix it:

Before I can find a solution the screens changes. They're there. The CEO, CMO, and right-hand executives.

It's a disaster:

And I'm in the middle of Jumanji. For forty-five minutes I present.

I try my best:

I'm at a 150% confidence the entire time.

If it doesn't work out — that's okay:

Here's what I do know: You can't always control what happens to you.

Here's how I stay proactive:

So I apply a five-minute rule.

Here's how I stay proactive:

I allow myself to be upset for 5 minutes. That's it.

For this reason — I see the bigger picture:

Because I got a lot of years ahead of me to close deals.

The learning lesson:

And the biggest ones you lose today? Will be the smallest in the long run.

YOU DON'T NEED EVERYTHING TO WIN

You can have a landing page that gets leads.

Then create an entire business out of it.

You don't even need a payment page.

Not even a thank-you page.

Because here's the secret — you just need to be good at starting relationships.

If you have a page that captures leads, you can filter through those leads and reach out to the most qualified via LinkedIn, personal email, or Facebook.

Get on video calls.

Meet them in person.

And develop a lot of rapport.

Sure, it's not the most scalable way.

But you know what's less scalable?

You not building a landing page because you don't know exactly how and when you'll make money from leads.

That's insane.

Most of my funnels never led to a payment page.

Still, I started.

And had thousands of conversations with prospects.

Then sold millions of dollar in services.

Without a single payment page.

If you're scared to get into online marketing because you can't build an entire funnel, then realize it's not a technical problem.

It's a psychology problem.

Your psychology problem.

How do you think people made sales before the internet?

They had conversations.

"Hey Josh, I'd love to write about your thoughts on X."

It's that simple.

The perfect funnel to make you a million dollars plus this year is great, but for 99 percent of people that won't happen.

You know what everyone can do?

They can build one landing page.

Then reach out with value.

And you can build a multi-million-dollar business this way. So if you're stuck because you can't do it all.

You don't have the marketing knowledge.

You don't have the technical chops.

Then realize this — you never needed it to be successful online in the first place.

You can have this benefit:

You can have a landing page that gets leads.

And leverage it to create this huge benefit:

Then create an entire business out of it.

You don't even need these commonly thought important pieces:

You don't even need a payment page. Not even a thank-you page.

For this simple reason:

Because here's the secret — you just need to be good at starting relationships.

Here's an example:

If you have a page that captures leads, you can filter through those leads and reach out to the most qualified via LinkedIn, personal email, or Facebook.

Here's how you can take advantage of it with simple steps:

Get on video calls. Meet them in person. And develop a lot of rapport.

It's not easy, but it's better than not taking action:

Sure, it's not the most scalable way. But you know what's less scalable? You not building a landing page because you don't know exactly how and when you'll make money from leads. That's insane.

I used this advice:

Most of my funnels never led to a payment page. Still, I started.

Here's the positive result:

And had thousands of conversations with prospects.
Then sold millions of dollar in services.

Without taking the normal route:

Without a single payment page.

This is what holds people back:

If you're scared to get into online marketing because you can't build an entire funnel, then realize it's not a technical problem.
*It's a psychology problem. **Your** psychology problem.*

This is how it worked before we had these systems:

How do you think people made sales before the internet? They had conversations. "Hey Josh, I'd love to write about your thoughts on X."
It's that simple.

Don't expect greatness right away:

The perfect funnel to make you a million dollars plus this year is great, but for 99 percent of people that won't happen.

Expect to get started:

You know what everyone can do? They can build one landing page. Then reach out with value.

You can get these results this way:

And you can build a multi-million-dollar business this way.

Don't let these self-conscious thoughts stop you:

So if you're stuck because you can't do it all. You don't have the marketing knowledge. You don't have the technical chops.

This is the learning lesson:

Then realize this — you never needed it to be successful online in the first place.

YOU DON'T NEED THE TRADITIONAL PATH

I don't have a mentor.

Haven't had one for four years.

I have people I admire such as Dennis Yu, but that's it.

What I've realized — some people learn better from experience.

If a mentor tells me not to put my hand on a hot stove, I'll do it anyways. I need to know.

Many people have a similar personality to me.

They place action over listening.

It works — I turned out fine. At least so far.

There's no clear path to success.

You don't need books, mentors, or an MBA.

Those are all secondary to grit, communication skills, and a willingness to be different.

The problem:

Most people place secondary success factors first.

"I need a MBA to show employers I'm competent."

"I need mentors before I start my company."

"I need venture capital for my idea."

Notice the trend here?

These people sound needy.

Neediness is unattractive for results.

What they should say,

"I'm just going to do it anyways."

"Let's see what happens."

You say these phrases enough times, and eventually, you get something right.

That's the personality trait that wins.

Because life doesn't need permission.

So don't act needy for it.

Controversial statement:

I don't have a mentor.

Dig into the controversy:

Haven't had one for four years.

There's a small exception:

I have people I admire such as Dennis Yu, but that's it.

Learning point most agree with:

What I've realized — some people learn better from experience.

Here's why this holds true using an example of myself:

If a mentor tells me not to put my hand on a hot stove, I'll do it anyways. I need to know.

I'm not alone:

Many people have a similar personality to me. They place action over listening.

Comedic break:

It works — I turned out fine. At least so far.

Here's what I've learned:

There's no clear path to success.

Second controversial learning:

You don't need books, mentors, or an MBA.

Here's why:

Those are all secondary to grit, communication skills, and a willingness to be different.

Here's the problem with self-conscious thoughts:

The problem: Most people place secondary success factors first. "I need a MBA to show employers I'm competent." "I need mentors before I start my company." "I need venture capital for my idea."

The negative bigger picture of these thoughts:

Notice the trend here? These people sound needy.
Neediness is unattractive for results.

Here's what they should think:

What they should say, "I'm just going to do it anyways."
"Let's see what happens."

Here's why:

You say these phrases enough times, and eventually, you get something right. That's the personality trait that wins.

The learning lesson:

Because life doesn't need permission. So don't act needy for it.

WHY I WORK WITH THE BEST

Hire senior people to avoid salespeople.

We had a $25K/month deal on the line yesterday.

I asked our new strategist, Melanie Balke, to lead it.

It's her first week.

And I didn't have a choice.

These meetings don't happen every day.

She needs to get the experience when she can.

With two hours beforehand, I realize this is the case.

So I asked her to lead the presentation.

She says "yes."

And again, it's only her first week with us.

She presents for the next hour and a half in front of five people on the client's team.

She covers seven different services and case studies.

By the end of the presentation, they're overjoyed.

And coming in today to discuss terms.

Here's what most agencies do —

They hire someone for half the cost.

Give them the same position.

Never bring them to high-deal sales meetings.

And take months to train them on basic marketing skills.

The funny part?

They pay less in overhead thinking they're winning.

Then the CEO realizes he's still the only person selling.

Here's what we do —
We hire experienced marketers who demand higher pay.

Then give them the opportunity to sell their experience to prospects.

The best part?

We no longer need salespeople.

And it's why we can scale $25K+/month meetings.

It's simple: I no longer have to be there.

It gets better — we have a 100 percent close rate for in-person meetings when competing against other agencies.

The main reason?

We bring the strategist who they'd work with to the meeting.

And they present.

Imagine if I told the prospect,

"I just gave you this nice presentation, but you won't be working with me. It'll be with this person who you don't know. We didn't include them in the meeting because they're too junior to sell their experience."

This is what it's like having salespeople at an agency.

More hand-offs.

More friction.

Want bigger deals?

You need account leads who can sell.

And a strong inbound machine.

That's it.

Bold statement favoring experience:

Hire senior people to avoid salespeople.

The stakes were high:

We had a $25K/month deal on the line yesterday.

— I put someone new to the team on it: ———

I asked our new strategist, Melanie Balke, to lead it. It's her first week.

— I had to do it: ———

And I didn't have a choice.

— For this reason: ———

These meetings don't happen every day.

— It's about them getting this benefit: ———

She needs to get the experience when she can.

— Under this deadline, I realized it: ———

With two hours beforehand, I realize this is the case.

— I took a chance on them: ———

So I asked her to lead the presentation. She says "yes."

┌─ A reminder that they're new to the team: ─────────────────

And again, it's only her first week with us.

┌─ Tough situation they get thrown into: ─────────────────

She presents for the next hour and a half in front of five people on the client's team. She covers seven different services and case studies.

┌─ They excelled: ─────────────────────────────────────

By the end of the presentation, they're overjoyed.
And coming in today to discuss terms.

┌─ Here's what our competitors do: ─────────────────────

Here's what most agencies do —

┌─ They cut corners: ───────────────────────────────────

They hire someone for half the cost.

Do the same thing I did:

Give them the same position.

But don't allow them to do this crucial part of their role:

Never bring them to high-deal sales meetings.

And then make it even worse with this:

And take months to train them on basic marketing skills.

Ironic that they think they're right:

The funny part? They pay less in overhead thinking they're winning.

Until they don't:

Then the CEO realizes he's still the only person selling. Here's what we do —

── We do the exact opposite in this unique way: ──

We hire experienced marketers who demand higher pay.

── Then give them this opportunity: ──

Then give them the opportunity to sell their experience to prospects.

── How it validates your first sentence: ──

The best part? We no longer need salespeople.

── Provide an example of validation: ──

And it's why we can scale $25K+/month meetings.

── As a result, this happens: ──

It's simple: I no longer have to be there.

— Here's how the benefit is more than what we —
   originally thought:

It gets better — we have a 100 percent close rate for in-person meetings when competing against other agencies.

— Here's why: ———————————————

The main reason? We bring the strategist who they'd work with to the meeting. And they present.

— Here's a tangible conversation of a negative example: —

Imagine if I told the prospect, "I just gave you this nice presentation, but you won't be working with me. It'll be with this person who you don't know. We didn't include them in the meeting because they're too junior to sell their experience."

— This is when it's against my statement in #1: ———

This is what it's like having salespeople at an agency.

You get these problems:

More hand-offs. More friction.

The learning lesson:

Want bigger deals? You need account leads who can sell. And a strong inbound machine. That's it.

HARD WORK PAYS OFF

Last week, I met a guy who sold his company for a 100 million dollars.

He's interested in working with us.

He pulled up to our office in a brand new car.

We went to the roof of our company to talk. It's a beautiful spot that overlooks all of Venice and most of Los Angeles.

There, he told us a story.

"I started my company at the same time my friend started his.

We both sold our companies for a hundred million dollars.

Here's the difference. He took funding.

Worked himself to death over five years.

You know how much he got out of it?"

I replied, "How much?"

"Three million."

"You know how much I got?"

"No idea."

He took a long pause, then grinned.

"All of it."

At that moment, I realized we made the right decision to bootstrap early on.

I've never seen anyone happier.

Recently, I met someone who had this huge accomplishment:

Last week, I met a guy who sold his company for a 100 million dollars.

They wanted to team up with us:

He's interested in working with us.

They met us in an impressive way:

He pulled up to our office in a brand new car.

We went to this exclusive location to talk:

We went to the roof of our company to talk. It's a beautiful spot that overlooks all of Venice and most of Los Angeles.

They explained a story with two parallels, high stakes, and huge benefits:

There, he told us a story. "I started my company at the same time my friend started his. We both sold our companies for a hundred million dollars. Here's the difference. He took funding. Worked himself to death over five years.

They explained how they got polar opposite results:

You know how much he got out of it?" I replied, "How much?"

The other guy didn't get much comparably:

"Three million." "You know how much I got?" "No idea." He took a long pause, then grinned. "All of it."

The learning lesson:

At that moment, I realized we made the right decision to bootstrap early on. I've never seen anyone happier.

ADOPT THIS ONE HABIT

I worked at four startups in two years.

They all failed.

And they were in four different markets: pharmaceuticals, real estate, crowdfunding, and the music industry.

So I founded my own company, an online publication.

A year later, that failed, too.

Then I became the VP of Marketing for a mobile app company that failed.

I lost all my money.

Had zero job prospects.

So I moved into my Dad's tiny apartment.

Without space, we slept in the same room.

I got a job as a copywriter that paid $12 an hour. It was awful.

At the same time, I made a decision to read for five hours every day on average.

This led to 170 books read over the next year about psychology, business, and marketing.

A few months after my copywriting gig, I had saved enough money to take a risk.

To work at a Facebook software company where I got paid half.

In eight months, I led their marketing.

Landed a few clients, then wrote a book about Facebook marketing.

Took that credibility, became the head of growth for a venture-backed company in San Francisco.

Then the head of growth for a 50-million-dollar VC firm.

Next the growth evangelist for one of the fast-growing SaaS companies.

Today, I'm the co-founder and CEO of a multi-million-dollar company.

Entirely bootstrapped.

The lesson — adopt the habit of persistence.

Persistent enough to where you'll pursue what you want no matter where you live, how much money you make, or connections you have.

If you want results, do what 99% of people won't.

I did a lot of work with risk:

I worked at four startups in two years.

None of it worked out:

They all failed.

I took the risks in different areas:

And they were in four different markets: pharmaceuticals, real estate, crowdfunding, and the music industry.

I moved on to take more risks under my own lead:

So I founded my own company, an online publication.

That didn't work out either:

A year later, that failed, too.

I tried again and failed:

Then I became the VP of Marketing for a mobile app company that failed.

I was left with these bad results:

I lost all my money. Had zero job prospects.

I was desperate and had to do this:

So I moved into my Dad's tiny apartment. Without space, we slept in the same room. I got a job as a copywriter that paid $12 an hour. It was awful. At the same time, I made a decision to read for five hours every day on average.

Tangible result:

This led to 170 books read over the next year about psychology, business, and marketing.

Even at the lowest point, I took another risk:

A few months after my copywriting gig, I had saved enough money to take a risk. To work at a Facebook software company where I got paid half.

It worked:

In eight months, I led their marketing.
Landed a few clients, then wrote a book about Facebook marketing.

I leveraged this positive outcome into another one:

Took that credibility, became the head of growth for a venture-backed company in San Francisco.

Then another one:

Then the head of growth for a 50-million-dollar VC firm.

Another:

Next the growth evangelist for one of the fast-growing SaaS companies.

And finally today:

Today, I'm the co-founder and CEO of a multi-million-dollar company. Entirely bootstrapped.

Here's what I realized:

The lesson — adopt the habit of persistence.

Here's an expansion on what I realized:

Persistent enough to where you'll pursue what you want no matter where you live, how much money you make, or connections you have.

Here's what I learned:

If you want results, do what 99% of people won't.

WHAT MAKES MY DAY

Here's what makes my day: When I call my Mom at 7 a.m.

Then wish her the best day ever.

My Mom has worked almost every day of her life.

Twelve-hour week days. Even many weekends.

When I was young, I wanted to help her.

I didn't know how.

My jobs paid me close to nothing.

Construction and dishwashing wasn't ideal for a family of five.

So I gave her something else beside money.

I gave her time.

Every morning she'd wake up at 6 a.m. to make coffee.

Then one day, I woke up at 5:30 a.m. to get it ready for her.

This way she could wake up to a hot cup.

No wait time.

She almost cried.

It was the first time someone really lended a hand.

I did it again.

And continued to do it for years.

Even through her divorce and depression.

It was a simple reminder that someone cared about her.

When I joined the workforce after college, I moved to San Francisco.

She no longer had that reminder.

Rather than stop.

I did something different.

I called her every morning to wish her the best day ever.

It's selfish — because it's the best gift I've given myself.

To understand how you can change someone's life with appreciation.

This vulnerable moment of caring for others makes me happy:

Here's what makes my day: When I call my Mom at 7 a.m.
Then wish her the best day ever.

Here's why I care for them:

My Mom has worked almost every day of her life. Twelve-hour week days. Even many weekends.

I couldn't do it before:

When I was young, I wanted to help her. I didn't know how.

Because of these tangible reasons:

My jobs paid me close to nothing.
Construction and dishwashing wasn't ideal for a family of five.

I decided to care for them in a non-traditional way:

So I gave her something else beside money. I gave her time.

I helped them in the simplest most meaningful way:

Every morning she'd wake up at 6 a.m. to make coffee. Then one day, I woke up at 5:30 a.m. to get it ready for her. This way she could wake up to a hot cup. No wait time. She almost cried.

The realization:

It was the first time someone really lended a hand.

I didn't stop:

I did it again.
And continued to do it for years.

Even through the hardest of times:

Even through her divorce and depression.

For this reason:

It was a simple reminder that someone cared about her.

— Then I faced this obstacle to continuing: —————

When I joined the workforce after college, I moved to San Francisco. She no longer had that reminder. Rather than stop. I did something different.

— So I changed up the way I did it: —————

I called her every morning to wish her the best day ever.

— It's not just helped them: —————

It's selfish — because it's the best gift I've given myself.

— Because of this learning experience: —————

To understand how you can change someone's life with appreciation.

TAKE THE UNTRADTIONAL ROUTE

— BEN LEE

SEO is dead.

Google doesn't care about your optimized blog post.

And Amazon isn't fooled by your search ranking hacks.

If you're thinking about paying someone to teach you SEO
— don't.

Save your money.

It's ancient history.

You'll be a 21st-century dinosaur.

What, then? Content.

The kind of stuff people actually love reading:
- Because it offers real, actionable value
- Because they'll tell all their friends about it
- Because it's just too damn interesting to click away
from

And social media.

Facebook, Linkedin, Instagram, Pinterest.

Putting yourself and your work out there in a genuine,
human way.

And finally, good 'ole fashioned paid advertising done right—
Ads with punchy copy selling real products that solve real
problems.

Where to start?

Learn from people who are doing it successfully.

Keep coming up with new and creative ideas.

Refine and clarify your message —

Until you build a real following.

The catch?

A classroom won't teach you how to do it.

And there are no shortcuts.

You'll have to put in the hours.

— Controversial short statement: —

SEO is dead.

— Explain why it's true using authorities: —

Google doesn't care about your optimized blog post.
And Amazon isn't fooled by your search ranking hacks.

Don't even bother learning why:

If you're thinking about paying someone to teach you SEO — don't. Save your money.

For these reasons:

It's ancient history. You'll be a 21st-century dinosaur.

Here's what works:

What, then? Content.

Here's why:

The kind of stuff people actually love reading: - Because it offers real, actionable value - Because they'll tell all their friends about it - Because it's just too damn interesting to click away from. And social media.

Here's how you should play the game:

Facebook, Linkedin, Instagram, Pinterest. Putting yourself and your work out there in a genuine, human way. And finally, good 'ole fashioned paid advertising done right —

With tangible examples:

Ads with punchy copy selling real products that solve real problems.

Here's how to jump in:

Where to start? Learn from people who are doing it successfully. Keep coming up with new and creative ideas. Refine and clarify your message — until you build a real following.

The twist — it won't be easy:

The catch? A classroom won't teach you how to do it. And there are no shortcuts. You'll have to put in the hours.

LEARN THE MOST VALUABLE LESSONS

— BEN LEE

I bought a small gaming studio instead of doing an MBA.

Then I spent $500K developing mobile games over 2 years.

And every single one of them failed.

They weren't addicting enough.

People stopped playing.

My team and I were crushed.

We couldn't look each other in the eye.

Not a day went by when I wasn't filled with doubt.

The irony?

Failure was the best thing that happened to me.

Without outside funding, we learned:
    - To handle all of our marketing in-house
    - To run the company as if we only have a one-month
      runway

And by seeing what people didn't like.

We understood what they loved.
Since then:
    - A hardware product we marketed raised over $2.5M
      on Kickstarter
    - Internal apps have gotten 100s of 5-star reviews.
    - We've launched a #1 game on Product Hunt

Instead of spending $200K on an MBA — I doubled down on my own company.

And got my masters. A masters in running a successful bootstrapped business.

Bottom line?

ROI is not only about making money on every dollar you spend.

Those lessons learned along the way?

Priceless.

I took an unconventional route of success:

I bought a small gaming studio instead of doing an MBA.

I invested everything into the decision:

Then I spent $500K developing mobile games over 2 years.

None of it worked out:

And every single one of them failed.

For these reasons:

They weren't addicting enough. People stopped playing.

The sad result with tangible examples:

My team and I were crushed. We couldn't look each other in the eye. Not a day went by when I wasn't filled with doubt.

It didn't matter — because we learned:

The irony? Failure was the best thing that happened to me. Without outside funding, we learned: - To handle all of our marketing in-house - To run the company as if we only have a one-month runway

The bigger picture learning lesson:

And by seeing what people didn't like. We understood what they loved.

These lessons helped us prevail afterwards with these wins:

Since then: - A hardware product we marketed raised over $2.5M on Kickstarter - Internal apps have gotten 100s of 5-star reviews. - We've launched a #1 game on Product Hunt

Rather than losing out on the traditional route, I won by making mistakes:

Instead of spending $200K on an MBA — I doubled down on my own company.

The valuable realization:

And got my masters. A masters in running a successful bootstrapped business. Bottom line?

The learning lesson:

ROI is not only about making money on every dollar you spend. Those lessons learned along the way? Priceless.

ENEMY TO PARTNER

— Ben Lee

I fired an engineer.

He outsourced all his work to China.

We tested him in Ruby, iOS, and JavaScript.

His work came back flawless.

And we spoke to three references.

Before us, he was employed at Cisco for more than five years.

My gut instinct didn't like him, but he checked all the boxes. And we were desperate for help.

When he started, he came up with every excuse to work remotely.

It was 2015, and everyone requested it.

Especially engineers.

We approved it.

Then we saw inconsistencies in the code.

He was leaving time stamps for UTC+8 which is China's time zone.

Then we saw a Trello card signed with a username handle of a Chinese pop star.

My CFO and I met him in a conference room.

We cut to the chase, "We have a check and separation agreement. We expect your full cooperation or we'll be handing this issue to the authorities."

He spilled the beans in less than five minutes — how he's never been a coder.

And outsourced his work to China for the past nine years.

In a weird way, he was almost proud of it.

We were stunned.

As a CEO, I had failed. I didn't trust my gut.

He fooled multinationals with multiple divisions for over nine years.

And then lasted two weeks with us.

It's a reality check I needed.

Talent comes and goes.

Intuition comes first.

┌─ **I stopped working with someone:** ─────────────┐

I fired an engineer.

└──┘

┌─── Because they took this controversial action: ───┐

He outsourced all his work to China.

├─── We vetted them and didn't see the negative signs: ───┤

We tested him in Ruby, iOS, and JavaScript. His work came back flawless. And we spoke to three references. Before us, he was employed at Cisco for more than five years.

├─── I had a feeling something was wrong: ───┤

My gut instinct didn't like him, but he checked all the boxes.

├─── We needed the help — it didn't matter: ───┤

And we were desperate for help.

├─── Even though they made controversial requests: ───┤

When he started, he came up with every excuse to work remotely.

─ We abided because we were accepting: ─────────

It was 2015, and everyone requested it. Especially engineers. We approved it.

─ Then the first problem occurred: ─────────

Then we saw inconsistencies in the code.
He was leaving time stamps for UTC+8 which is China's time zone.

─ Then a second problem: ─────────

Then we saw a Trello card signed with a username handle of a
Chinese pop star.

─ We had a meeting with them: ─────────

My CFO and I met him in a conference room.

─ Told them it was over: ─────────

We cut to the chase, "We have a check and separation agreement. We expect
your full cooperation or we'll be handing this issue to the authorities."

They confessed:

He spilled the beans in less than five minutes — how he's never been a coder. And outsourced his work to China for the past nine years.

They took delight in their actions:

In a weird way, he was almost proud of it. We were stunned.

It was my fault:

As a CEO, I had failed. I didn't trust my gut.

Even though they had tricked many high-level people:

He fooled multinationals with multiple divisions for over nine years.

They didn't last long with us:

And then lasted two weeks with us. It's a reality check I needed.

— The learning lesson: —————————————————

Talent comes and goes. Intuition comes first.

KEEP UP WITH CHANGING SETTINGS

— BEN LEE

On my plane ride, I saw a mom about to have a nervous breakdown.

Her kids were glued to their screens.

And one was complaining.

The mom looked at her husband, "Honey, she's missing her iPad"

I watched the dad rummage through their luggage.

"Give me one second."

You could feel the tension.

I'm scared for this younger generation.

I'm grateful to have been born when I was.

I skateboarded, rollerbladed, and read books before the iPad.

Many kids won't experience the world like many of us have.

Most of their experiences will come through screens.

I would rather exercise without a VR headset.

And not spend my weekends playing video games.

The most successful people I know don't let screens control them.

— Here's the harsh truth about this new setting: —

Many kids won't experience the world like many of us have.
Most of their experiences will come through screens.

— It's better to do these things than these things: —

I would rather exercise without a VR headset.
And not spend my weekends playing video games.

— Here's why with credible examples: —

The most successful people I know don't let screens control them.
Warren Buffett doesn't check his Slack channel every day.
Let alone his Berkshire Hathaway e-mail account.

— Here's a completely different setting with the —
opposite happening:

I've been visiting Uruguay for six years.
Fashion, tech, and music trends are delayed here.

— Here are the tangible results: —

Their kids still read books, paint, and talk in person.
It makes me sad that I don't see this in the U.S.

The realization:

If we want to lead future generations. We need to accept one thing: They're growing up in an entirely different world. And it doesn't exist offline. It exists online.

The learning lesson:

It's our job to show them real relationships are built on handshakes. Not on Instagram likes.

LEADERSHIP IS A CHOICE

— BEN LEE

I take seven Uber rides a day.

They make me sit in the front seat.

In Uruguay, the taxi drivers hate Uber drivers.

They'll slash their tires.

And even resort to physical violence.

To stay under the radar, they don't use the Uber stickers.

And don't put people in the backseat.

Uber messed up the drug trade — and it hit some important pockets.

Especially taxis that were once used as drug mules.

I know all of this because I talk to my drivers about their culture.

The drivers don't meet many Americans so they're always game.

As a founder, I take every opportunity to learn.

My Spanish is far from perfect.

This allows me to practice.

The city I live in, Montevideo, is so small.

I had the same driver twice in 48 hours.

That's how I met Felipe, an Uber entrepreneur who wants to create an app.

It would help tourists overcome cultural hurdles.

There's a lot of smart people here.

And business opportunities.

The only way I see them is by immersing myself.

I'm a CEO, leading a team of designers and developers in another country.

It's humbling.

It's scary.

It reminds me that leadership is a choice.

Not a job title.

─── **I take this strange action:** ───────────────

I take seven Uber rides a day.

─── **It gets even weirder:** ────────────────────

They make me sit in the front seat.

It's a different culture:

In Uruguay, the taxi drivers hate Uber drivers. They'll slash their tires. And even resort to physical violence. To stay under the radar, they don't use the Uber stickers.

That's why #2 makes sense:

And don't put people in the backseat.

It's because technology disruption has had a big impact:

Uber messed up the drug trade - and it hit some important pockets. Especially taxis that were once used as drug mules.

I learned this because I take every extra effort to learn about others' cultures:

I know all of this because I talk to my drivers about their culture. The drivers don't meet many Americans so they're always game. As a founder, I take every opportunity to learn.

It helps me in indirect ways as well:

My Spanish is far from perfect. This allows me to practice.

The culture here allows you to meet inspiring people like this person who wants to create this product/ service:

The city I live in, Montevideo, is so small. I had the same driver twice in 48 hours. That's how I met Felipe, an Uber entrepreneur who wants to create an app. It would help tourists overcome cultural hurdles. There's a lot of smart people here. And business opportunities.

The only way to see these opportunities is to jump in:

The only way I see them is by immersing myself.

I'm not in my culture and have a lot of responsibility:

I'm a CEO, leading a team of designers and developers in another country. It's humbling. It's scary.

The learning lesson:

It reminds me that leadership is a choice. Not a job title.

VALUE YOUR TIME

At some point — you get it.

When a prospect tries to turn a thirty-minute call into a two-hour call, you tell them "anytime after this half hour and I'll need to charge you for a consultation."

Asks for you to provide a full analysis of their business before you work together, you say "no."

Says, "You need to earn my business," you hang up.

Asks to meet at your office, you say "no."

Wants five references, you move on.

The only person who cares about your time?

That's you.

Nobody else.

90 percent of our clients never asked for a full audit of their business.

90 percent of our clients kept calls short and to the point.

90 percent of our clients didn't meet at our office beforehand.

90 percent of our clients never asked for a reference.

The other ten percent?

They've wasted 90 percent of our time.

That's the reality of sales.

When you realize there's a difference between prospects and buyers.

It hits you:

At some point — you get it.

When someone tries to take advantage of you in these ways:

When a prospect tries to turn a thirty-minute call into a two-hour call, you tell them "anytime after this half hour and I'll need to charge you for a consultation." Asks for you to provide a full analysis of their business before you work together, you say "no." Says, "You need to earn my business," you hang up. Asks to meet at your office, you say "no" Wants five references, you move on.

The only person who will fight it:

The only person who cares about your time? That's you. Nobody else.

Because this is where most of the benefit comes from:

90 percent of our clients never asked for a full audit of their business.
90 percent of our clients kept calls short and to the point.
90 percent of our clients didn't meet at our office beforehand.
90 percent of our clients never asked for a reference.

The rest of it comes from here:

The other ten percent? They've wasted 90 percent of our time.
That's the reality of sales.

Tie into previous sentence and overall realization:

When you realize there's a difference between prospects and buyers.

FOCUS ON LONGEVITY

I had a brilliant talk with Noah Kagan. The one thing I learned: You don't own anything on the internet. Not even your email list.

If email dies, so will your list. If something bigger than the internet arrives — *and it will* — then most businesses will fail.

The only difference between entrepreneurs who survive in the long run is they stay nimble and test often.

Businesses die every day because they over-invest into a channel without saving budget for testing. That's why they have no lifetime value. None.

Can a business turn off one traction channel without going broke?

Can it turn off two without going broke?

How about three?

Probably not.

99% of businesses would disappear overnight.

As a result, the most scalable marketing model doesn't depend on the internet — it's offline. It's get-togethers, workshops, and events. A better word for it? Community. It'll be there tomorrow, five years from now, and even fifty years.

Here's what won't: Everything you see online today.

As a result, the most scalable marketing channels — if you want to build a 50-year brand — happen in person.

It may take longer. It may be more expensive.

But in the long run? You'll win every time.

If you want to build an empire — don't focus on speed like most founders.

Focus on longevity.

I met with an influencer and learned this hard lesson:

I had a brilliant talk with Noah Kagan. The one thing I learned: You don't own anything on the internet. Not even your email list.

Here's why this problem is true:

*If email dies, so will your list. If something bigger than the internet arrives — **and it will** — then most businesses will fail.*

Here's how you survive:

The only difference between entrepreneurs who survive in the long run is they stay nimble and test often.

Don't do this:

Businesses die every day because they over-invest into a channel without saving budget for testing. That's why they have no lifetime value. None.

How you know whether you'll overcome the problem:

Can a business turn off one traction channel without going broke?
Can it turn off two without going broke? How about three? Probably not.
99% of businesses would disappear overnight.

The realization and solutions:

As a result, the most scalable marketing model doesn't depend on the internet — it's offline. It's get-togethers, workshops, and events. A better word for it? Community. It'll be there tomorrow, five years from now, and even fifty years.

Here's the opposite:

Here's what won't: Everything you see online today.

Here's what you need to do and keep in mind to survive:

As a result, the most scalable marketing channels — if you want to build a 50-year brand — happen in person. It may take longer. It may be more expensive. But in the long run? You'll win every time.

The learning lesson:

If you want to build an empire — don't focus on speed like most founders. Focus on longevity.

WHY I'M WEALTHY

I consider myself wealthy.

I did even when I was broke living in my Dad's tiny apartment.

Because I owned the most expensive gift in the world: clarity.

I knew exactly what I wanted to do.

Several years ago, I wrote down that I wanted to build a 100-million-dollar company and write a best-selling fiction and non-fiction book.

Today, I run a multi-million-dollar agency.

And I've published four books.

Here's the thing —
I still haven't hit my goals.

Even after three years.

But I'm closer than ever.

Because clarity creates reality.

And when you have the confidence that you'll build your dream —
You're the wealthiest person in the world.

I had this quality even when most people wouldn't think so:

I consider myself wealthy.
I did even when I was broke living in my Dad's tiny apartment.

For this reason:

Because I owned the most expensive gift in the world: clarity.
I knew exactly what I wanted to do.

A long time ago I made a promise:

Several years ago, I wrote down that I wanted to build a 100-million-dollar company and write a best-selling fiction and non-fiction book.

Today, I'm closer with these tangible accomplishments:

Today, I run a multi-million-dollar agency. And I've published four books. Here's the thing —

— Not there, but close: —————————————

I still haven't hit my goals. Even after three years. But I'm closer than ever.

— For this reason: ———————————————————

Because clarity creates reality.
And when you have the confidence that you'll build your dream —

— It'll create this outcome — tie back to #1: ————————

You're the wealthiest person in the world.

Hey [community member names - ex. fit founders].
Comment below with your [relevant - ex. favorite workout].

Let the follow train begin.
Drop your [social media platform] profile link below.

What are you selling?
Drop it in the comments below!

What are you selling below $99?
Drop it in the comments below :)

What can you give the community for free?
Drop it in the comments below :)

Who are you looking to partner with?
We've added thousands of more [community name] to
the community over the [time span].
Let's make some connections

Hey [community name],
I got a question for you: How do you focus?
Drop a comment below

Who are you looking to partner with to help take you
to the next level? [list relevant positions here - ex.
founders, companies].
Let's build relationships. Comment below.

What's one decision that changed your entire career path?
Let's hear it

What are your goals for this week?
Let's hear it .

What's motivating you today to crush it?
Let's hear it

Hey **[community name]**,
What was your biggest adrenaline rush moment as an entrepreneur?
Comment below

Looking to hire a [**relevant positions**]?
Make your pitch in the comments

Hey [**community name**],
What did you accomplish this week?
Let's hear it

Are you *already* a [**relevant position to the group — ex. fit founder**]?

Ask. Me. Anything.
Comment below.

Where are you from?

Who helped get you to where you are today?

What did you do before [X]?

"No force on earth can stop an idea whose time has come."
— Victor Hugo

To learn more about BAMF Media, please visit our website here:
https://www.bamf.media/grow

ABOUT THE AUTHOR

Josh is the co-founder of BAMF Media, the former head of growth for three companies, including the VC firm, GrowthX. He's also the former evangelist for a couple of the fastest growing SaaS companies, including Autopilot and Mixmax.

His previous repertoire of books include:

› **BAMF BIBLE**
› LinkedIn Influencer
› Content Machine

On top of that, Josh is a Top Quora Writer of 2017 & 2018, founded and leads one of the top communities for marketers and founders (20,000+ members).

Many people know Josh as the guy who broke LinkedIn's algorithm racking up 200 million views in six months on the platform.

Josh's marketing work has been featured in Reuters, Forbes, Entrepreneur, Mashable, Inc., and BuzzFeed. Today, he gives keynotes around the world on marketing and entrepreneurship.

He also has this epic picture with Mark Zuckerberg.

CPSIA information can be obtained
at www.ICGtesting.com
Printed in the USA
BVHW030939150719
553471BV00007B/196/P

9 780995 110380